1/6295

D0479135

9.95
8.95
7.95
6.95
5.95
4.95
3.95

The Sea:

Selections from the
First International Miyuki Delica
Challenge

Published by Caravan Beads, Inc.
Portland, Maine

Copyright © 1998 Caravan Beads, Inc.
Published 1998 by Caravan Beads, Inc.
All rights reserved. No part of this publication may be reproduced,
stored in a retrieval system, or transmitted, in any form or by any means—
electronic, mechanical, recording, or otherwise—
without the prior written permission of Caravan Beads, Inc.

Edited by Barry Kahn
Color Photography by Howell, Ltd.
Printed in the United States of America

FIRST PRINTING: MAY, 1998

ISBN 0-9664319-0-1

Front cover: detail from Ocean Artisan by Jane Davis
Back Cover, left: detail of Moisson de la Mer by Gale Tomlinson
Back Cover, right: detail of FantaSea by Margo Field

Delica® is a registered trademark of Miyuki Shoji Co., Ltd.
Caravan Beads® is a registered trademark of Caravan Beads, Inc.

CONTENTS

Foreword and Acknowledgements   *Barry Kahn*

The photographs in this book show the work of beaders from all over the United States as well as Australia, England and Japan. Each photograph is accompanied by text from the artist who created the pictured work. Binding them together is the 1st International Miyuki Delica Challenge theme— the sea—and the use of Miyuki Delicas, small cylinder-shaped glass beads, to create the works. We have, naturally, included photographs of all the winning entries. The other photographs were selected to show the wide range of beadwork entered in the competition. As we received the entries last summer, prior to the judging, we were amazed, amused, inspired, and astonished by the imagination, patience, and talent they revealed. Our hope is that these photographs and the words of the artists will inspire you to try beadwork if you never have, and to aspire to new challenges if you are already a beader.

Many people contributed to the success of the 1st International Miyuki Delica Challenge. My heartfelt thanks to:

Isabel Jones, who made the original suggestion.

Penny Taylor-Wallace, who emailed me invaluable advice, practical suggestions, and helped revise and proofread the rules and entry form.

Masayoshi Katsuoka, President of Miyuki Shoji Co., Ltd., for inventing Delicas in the first place, for encouraging us, and for agreeing to be one of the jurors. Thanks also to Mrs. Katsuoka, especially for her language skills which were so helpful.

Carolyn Mitchell, who with my wife, Jean, co-founded Caravan Beads. In addition to being on the jury, Carolyn and her husband, Joe, offered their Georgetown, Maine home as a location for the judging and spent many hours ensuring that the weekend would be a success. Salt water lapping at the edge of the yard created the perfect setting for the competition theme.

Alice Scherer, Director of the Center for the Study of Beadwork, the third juror. The breadth and depth of her knowledge made her an invaluable asset to the jurying process.

Lora Winslow, who designed the famous limited-edition "Delicas Rule" pin for those who entered the competition.

Our employees, who helped in innumerable ways to keep all systems going while we added the extra work of the competition to their already busy days. They are worth their weight in Delicas!

And last but not at all least, the bead artists who submitted entries to this first-time competition.

Thanks are also due to those who helped with this book:

Carolyn Mitchell, Ros Arienti, Lora Winslow, Pamela Clark, Jean Kahn, Melissa Ross, and others who read the manuscript and helped with the editing.

Paul Howell, of Howell, Ltd., and his fine staff, for their excellent digital photography.

Bonnie Bousquet-Smith for her assistance with the instructions.

Judging the 1st International Miyuki Delica Challenge
September 19-20, 1997
Barry Kahn

The three judges were Alice Scherer of the Center for the Study of Beadwork in Portland, Oregon, Masayoshi Katsuoka, President of Miyuki Shoji Co., Ltd., and Carolyn Mitchell, co-founder of Caravan Beads, Inc. The judging took place at the Mitchells' summer home on a tidal cove in Georgetown, Maine. On Friday, September 19th, we unpacked and arranged all the entries for the first round of judging. Once everything was organized, lighting adjusted, and pens and note pads handed out, the judges discussed the criteria to use in judging the entries.

Their list included:

- Technical merit: variety of techniques, quality of execution, technical challenge
- Design and use of color
- Originality
- Adherence to the theme of the sea and success in developing the theme
- Best use of Delicas

This is a quick summary. As an observer I could see that the judges evaluated the entries in a variety of ways: comparing and contrasting similar pieces; evaluating individual pieces against abstract standards of design, technique; and so on. It was a complex process and one which evolved as they moved through the judging process and the number of remaining entries diminished.

Once the basic criteria were agreed upon, the first elimination round began. (There were eighty-two entries in all.) During the first round, entries were examined to see how well they adhered to the competition theme of the sea. Those that didn't—and there were a few—were put aside. This set the pattern for the next few rounds. At each pass, each judge would list those pieces which, due to weaknesses in one or more of the listed criteria, he or she felt should be eliminated. Then they compared notes and if all three judges agreed, the piece in question was removed from the judging tables. This system worked reasonably well at first, but slowed down as the quality of the remaining pieces made them increasingly difficult to eliminate. After a few rounds about half the pieces had been removed and we all agreed to stop for dinner and continue on Saturday morning.

Judging resumed Saturday after breakfast. We had extra tables set up and as entries were eliminated, Mrs. Katsuoka and I removed them and rearranged the remaining pieces. One of the more amusing and touching (to me, at least) parts of the process was that individual judges would insist on retaining certain pieces that they knew would not last into the final round. "I know we'll take it out on the next round," someone would say, "but it's so pretty I just want to keep it here a little longer." Eventually—the 6th or 7th round—there remained about 20 finalists. At this point the decision-making slowed to a crawl. Some time was spent discussing weak points of a few of these, but in each case at least one judge would say, "I know, but I'm not willing to see it go yet." Finally Alice Scherer suggested that each judge, without discussion, make a list of his or her top five picks to see if there was agreement on which ones might be the prize winners. This was agreed to and after about ten minutes, they compared notes. Interestingly, only Neva Wuerfel's entry received votes from all three judges, and she eventually received first prize. We then did some semifinal rearranging, putting the probable top six pieces on one table and the rest of the finalists nearby. The judges were then able to eliminate (with a LOT of moaning and sad feelings) a few more of the finalists. Further discussion and balloting followed which yielded agreement on the 2nd prize and arguments over 3rd. Three or four entries seemed to deserve Honorable Mentions, and each judge selected his or her favorite for the individual Judge's Choice awards. We then took a break to clear our minds and vision, followed by the final hour-long push to make the toughest decisions.

Making the final choices was very difficult. At this stage any small flaws in technique, design, color choices, etc. were pointed out, entries were moved around so they could be examined side by side, and so on. In the end there was a deadlock for 3rd place. Once it became clear that it really was a deadlock and that no amount of further discussion was likely to break it, I stepped in and offered another 3rd place prize. That cleared the way for agreement on the three Honorable Mentions, which in turn made it relatively easy for the judges to pick their Judge's Choice pieces. One question remained: what about *Sorry Charlie*®? This entry had been an instant hit with our employees and the judges also felt it deserved recognition. Wishing to encourage humor in beading, we finally decided to create a new award, the Employees' Choice Award, which will also be an optional award in future competitions.

What mattered to the judges?

Finishing and attention to detail were critical. In the final rounds, the judges eliminated a number of otherwise wonderful pieces because of flaws in finishing. Some of the prize winners also lost their chance to receive higher awards for the same reason. To quote from Carol Wilcox Wells in her book, *Creative Bead Weaving*:

> . . .It is so very important that every bead be right. Every element is part of the whole, and if the finished work is to be spectacular, so should every individual bead. The same is true of finishing a piece. If you have spent hours weaving a brooch or evening purse, then it deserves a carefully-attached finding or a well-sewn lining.

Attention to the theme was critical. Several entries were disqualified because the judges felt they did not adhere to the theme of the sea. The more tenuous or unclear the connection to the theme, the sooner the entry was likely to be removed from consideration.

These judges awarded originality, imagination, and ambition. Many of the entries which didn't make the final rounds were technically well done and attractive but simply not as imaginative or as challenging to make as those which received awards.

In closing, I wish to report that the judges repeatedly expressed their pleasure at the variety of pieces entered and at the overall quality of the work. I can only echo their sentiments—well done, everybody!

In addition to the purely in-your-face physical appeal of beads, I find continuing fascination and satisfaction in their universality. What can an archaeologist expect to find in a tomb of any era virtually any place on the planet? What did Columbus carry with him knowing their value would transcend the need for a common language? What do so many of us bring home as keepsakes of our own travels to far away places or just from a walk on the beach? Some small treasure strung on a cord worn in appreciation of its beauty, its rarity, its magic, its symbolism, its sheer irresistibility: a bead . . . or a bunch of beads.

The entries in the 1st Miyuki Delica Challenge were a magnificent illustration of the awesome scope of the bead world. To qualify, the artists used a single kind of bead, indeed a single brand of bead. Many used the same or similar colors, the same or similar techniques, to present the same or similar images. Yet no piece was the same or similar to another. The competition affirmed an essential truth known to beaders and, more widely, to artists in any medium the world over: limitations are entirely within the individual; the smallest opportunity for creativity affords a sea of possibilities.

The sea theme was Barry Kahn's idea. For those of you who have not dealt with Barry directly, imagine the Energizer bunny with a close-cropped beard, a telephone receiver perpetually tucked under his chin, one hand attached to a computer mouse, the other performing seventeen distinct tasks simultaneously (his mind can juggle more, but physical limitations happen). This man is blessed/cursed with super-human energy, a gargantuan thirst for new challenges, the shortest learning curve imaginable, and a family wonderfully resigned to all of the above. The production of this book (at least 97% his effort) is but a single Delica in his cranial warehouse.

The sea was a perfect choice to underscore the universality of beads. It brought Japan and Maine together on many levels from the mundane bottom-line driven world of commerce to the sudden intake of breath associated with being in close contact with works of inestimable talent and beauty. Mr. and Mrs. Katsuoka were appreciative guests, at ease in our rambling old farmhouse which must have felt quite far removed from the refinement of Japan. Aided by Mrs. Katsuoka's translation skills, we were increasingly bonded by our mutual appreciation for our coastal setting, the pleasure of good company, the artistry of the works before us, and the difficulty of judging especially as it dawned on us that every entrant deserved recognition and we were charged with identifying so very few "winners."

Fortunately, Alice Scherer had experience with this dilemma and she was invaluably effective in moving us along the arduous path of decision-making. Barry and our dedicated Caravan Beads staff had done a super job of organizing and trouble-shooting in advance which made the judging weekend proceed amazingly smoothly. Finally, my husband Joe and daughter Emily pitched into kitchen detail with zeal helping to keep the judges well-fed and worry-free of details not associated with the work of judging. What could have been a time of difficulty and tension turned out to be one of shared pleasure and rewarding recognition of the universal appeal of beads and the artists who work with them.

Masayoshi Katsuoka

I was honored to be a judge for the 1st Miyuki Delica Challenge sponsored and hosted by Caravan Beads. I wish to express my gratitude to the many people from the United States and other countries who participated in this competition. To see their wonderful creations made the long trip from Japan to Portland, Maine, very worthwhile.

I would also like to offer my respect and gratitude to Barry Kahn. It takes courage, passion, and strong organizational skills to successfully put together a new event such as this design competition. My thanks also to Mr. and Mrs. Mitchell who offered the use of their serene, lovely home for the judging.

It was a great experience for me to be a judge. However, the judging was very difficult because there were so many exquisite works. Alice, Carolyn, and I debated a lot over many of the pieces. In the end I think we judged fairly.

One little bead, a mere dot, joined with others becomes a line, then a surface and finally a beautiful creation. . . I looked at the gorgeous entries to the competition and felt great joy at being a creator of beads.

Alice Scherer

From a subterranean beginning, the field of contemporary beadwork has blossomed luxuriously. Today, three magazines devote themselves entirely, or nearly so, to contemporary beadwork, and several others regularly run articles on the subject. From no exhibitions at all, we are now in an era when there are several shows of beadwork each year. And where bead artists once rarely knew of even three others working in this medium, now many dozens are famous worldwide for their work and a network has been created, linking artists one to another.

One reason this has been possible is because manufacturers and distributors have been willing to help support the work of promoting this field. Early on, the Czech seed bead makers and their American distributors were instrumental in helping *The New Beadwork* come to fruition. The Miyuki Shoji Company and its president, Mr. Katsuoka, have been a part, not only of this project, but of the book *Beaded Amulet Purses*, which showcased the work of twenty-four artists from a narrow slice of the field whose work had been almost entirely unseen.

It has been my deepest pleasure over the last twenty-five years to watch the growth of beading. For years, Joyce Scott was virtually the only person working three dimensionally. Now dozens do. Where pieces were formerly comprised of one technique, maybe two, now a rich variety of techniques form various parts of a work, with the artist using whichever technique will best do the job. Today's beadworkers are more skilled and more creative than most of their predecessors, and have more knowledge about beadwork in general. We are in the age of information explosion and the world of beadwork is no exception. Each new project, whether that of an individual beadworker, or someone promoting the field, raises the bar of what's possible for us all. It's an exciting time and I am thrilled to be involved with it.

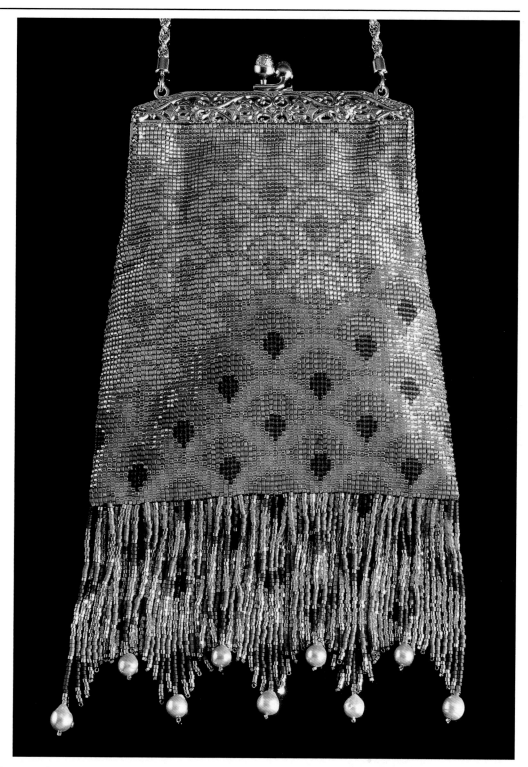

Mrs. Hiroko Imai lives in Yokohama, Japan. She is a member of and instructor in the Delica Bead Loom Association of Japan as well as the President of the Creative Beadweaving Club which she founded. Her entry, titled "Cocktail Bag," evokes the traditional Japanese design of a blue ocean wave. The bag is intended for use with either Japanese or Western style dress.

Gloria McClain

Most of my formal training has been in the graphic and fine arts. I started water color at the age of eight. I was always good at realism, so I assumed I would earn a living as an illustrator. To prepare for this career, I studied commercial art at the Dallas Art Institute. When I arrived in New York at age nineteen I was told that with my talent I should be doing faux finishes. Consequently I took a position as a gilder and for the next ten years worked at gilding and faux finishes. During the past three years my personal artwork has focused primarily on woodworking. I have also been studying silversmithing and gem cutting and hope to use that knowledge in future pieces.

Although I have collected seed beads for years, I never made anything with them. The 1st Miyuki Delica Challenge provided me with the motivation to complete my first project even though I was unable to use any of my collection in it.

From the moment I heard the theme of the contest the only clear picture that came to mind was Katsushika Hokusai's "Under the Waves of Kanagawa." It has always been one of my favorite works. I did worry that it was too popular and someone else might do the same one but as I tried to think of others it was the only one that I really cared for. Having decided what to make, I realized that I did not own a copy of the woodcut. I was lucky to find a set of postcards that contained a copy.

After much thought I decided to use an embroidery technique. I started by making a drawing of the completed project. Next I transferred the actual beading design to unbleached muslin and did an ink wash with the desired colors. Using what I have always called a back stitch, I applied the beads in the directions which flowed with the design. I started with the foreground and worked my way to the back—just the opposite of painting with oils. After the beading was completed and black velvet applied to the back, I added the trimming and fringe. The frame was modeled on Japanese meditation chimes a friend had given me. The only part of the design I changed were the straight posts. I decided the twisted posts would compliment the trimming on the tapestry.

Emiko Matsutsuyu

At California State University, Hayward, I studied portrait sculpture which was my first love before basketry and weaving. I have been a basket weaver since 1985 and belong to the Bay Area Basket Makers. In 1994 fifteen of us rented a cabin at South Lake Tahoe for a weekend of basket making. While there we saw some Washoe Indian basket makers exhibiting and selling beaded baskets. I couldn't afford one, so I decided right then that I would learn to bead. Later that year I started to weave what I call mini-baskets. They were embellished with seed beads and worn as necklaces.

In November, 1995, someone sent me an announcement for a Chrysanthemum Ball art contest. It called for any art form depicting the chrysanthemum. Because I love the spider mum, I decided to give it a try with white seed beads. (This was before I discovered Delicas!) In order to study its growth pattern, I went to a florist shop and purchased one spider mum. I also wanted to be sure to create the correct leaf formation.

This was my first attempt at loom weaving. I wove the leaves by warping the loom with fine copper wire, and with a book alongside the loom instructing me, I completed the leaves. I assembled the single bloom and inserted it in a bamboo vase circled by fine black bamboo.

The result was unbelievable. People attending the Chrysanthemum Ball voted to award me the first prize of $450.

The decision to attempt beading *Sea Kelp* was made after visiting various aquarium shops and looking at tropical fish. I had seen a beautiful photograph in a book as well. In addition I knew that the Monterey Bay Aquarium, a three-hour drive from where I live, features a three-story-high kelp forest. Rebecca Lewis, a fellow basket maker, generously offered to drive me there so I could study the kelp and take snapshots of the kelp forest as a guide for assembly of the kelp pods and fronds. Another basket maker, Gail Ruvalcaba, specializes in seaweed basketry. She gathers various kinds of seaweed. The dried brown gas floats were given to me by Gail.

To make the pods or floats, I painted the dried brown pods white. I then used peyote stitch with yellow Delicas to cover them. They are supported by fine steel rods. The fronds of kelp were loom woven with fine copper wire to create curvature. Copper strips support them. The floats and fronds are attached to an abalone shell. Finally, I attached the abalone shell to a hardwood base to complete my presentation of *Sea Kelp*.

In closing, I would like to let readers know that age should not be a deterrent to beading. I am seventy-six years of age and use an Opti-visor to assist me in counting and picking up my Delica beads. It helps for threading the needle also.

Between 1972 and 1981, Emiko Matsutsuyu was commissioned to make a number of bronze portrait busts in Hayward and Oakland, California. Her work is also in many private collections and she has participated in many museum and gallery shows annually since 1987. Her art training at California State University, Hayward, also included working with porcelain and metal sculpture.

Mary Winters-Meyer *3rd Prize*

I began beading in the summer of 1996. I had been meeting with friends at a local needlework shop every Saturday, and one day picked up a small beaded bracelet kit. From there I progressed to bead stringing, and then to seed bead work, which I enjoy the most. I've also dabbled in wirework, but find it hard on my wrists.

Last February I had the opportunity to attend the Bead Workshop in Paradise in Sarasota, Florida. Carol Wilcox Wells taught her sculptural peyote basket. Lydia Borin, the BeadWrangler, also taught at the seminar. She combines fiber art with beads.

Beading takes up most of my time when I'm not working or sleeping! I'm currently working on a pattern book which will include designs for at least three amulet bags and matching accessories. The pattern uses a new beading technique which I've developed. My article in the February 1998 issue of <u>Bead and Button</u> features this technique as well. I would like to get involved in teaching, but have not yet done so except for some one-on-one sessions with bead friends. *Seascape Surprises,* my entry in the 1st Miyuki Delica Challenge, is my first piece to receive an award.

Here are the techniques used in *Seascape Surprises*:

* Background and top of form - all done in single peyote, both flat and tubular
* Fish - square stitch
* Sandy bottom - peyote
* Coral - various techniques, including flat peyote, tubular peyote, branched fringe, square stitch, freeform embellishment, and right angle weave
* Seaweed - various branched fringe techniques
* Whitecaps - freeform embellishment
* Sea urchin - freeform embellishment with tight spiky fringe
* Bottom straps - flat peyote

My initial inspiration for *Seascape Surprises* came while visiting Florida last February. I had read about the Delica Challenge and was interested, but I didn't really have any ideas about what I would do. Seeing all the seaside artwork really put my imagination into high gear. I loved the murals on the walls of buildings along the highway. I spent hours roaming through the art shops in Key West. I even bought a book on coral reef fish which I later used extensively as a reference for my entry. I came back from Florida with so many ideas that two months passed before I could get my mind settled down enough to start beading!

I was also inspired by a bead class I took with Lydia Borin. Her class project involved making a bead-embellished fiber amulet bag without a pattern to follow. Before taking this class, I was hesitant to work without some sort of pattern in front of me. I would spend hours trying to design pieces using bead graph paper which never turned out quite right. This class taught me how to "go with the flow" of the project and let the design elements combine in unexpected ways. The results were surprisingly complex and beautiful and could never have been achieved through structured planning. From the start, I wanted to play with how light altered the quality of beads. It reminded me of the play of light on water, and how light affected the color of the water as it passed through. I made rough sketches before I started beading the Challenge entry, but set them aside when the project and my imagination refused to fit the sketches.

My initial idea was a simple flat peyote piece that could be mounted on a slanted one-piece plastic picture frame. I was worried, however, that the heat from a candle to backlight the piece might burn the plastic. Some time later, at a craft fair, I saw a booth with glass bricks decorated with ribbons and silk flowers. A candle shone through and highlighted the arrangements. I modified my original idea to a peyote form which would cover a glass brick. I decided to leave the back of the piece open so that the candle (which I pictured glowing through the beads from the back) would not burn the threads holding the beads in place. It wasn't until I was halfway done with the piece that I realized that leaving the back uncovered created a wonderful "aquarium" look in the finished piece.

The whole design of *Seascape Surprises* was freeform. Design decisions were made as I worked, and pieces of the design evolved as I went along. For example, I originally planned to use both opaque and translucent beads in the peyote cover, with the opaque beads forming fish silhouettes. Once I started working on the project, however, I found that light not only passed through the translucent beads, but also between the opaque ones, and the silhouettes were lost in the light. I modified my original idea, and beaded the fish as more colorful embellishments on top of the peyote base rather than being a part of it. I also tried several different stitches to get a "wave" effect on the top of the piece, but none looked good. Instead I created the smaller, ripple-like whitecaps. I intended to have more fish but they turned out bigger than expected. I would have loved to put in two or three sea horses among the coral, but had to be content with just one.

The straps on the bottom of the brick were also a modification of the original idea. As I worked on the project, I found that the cover would pull up off the form very easily, and decided to add the straps to keep it from coming off by accident. I thought about making it a single permanent strap, but decided that wouldn't be a good idea in case the brick base ever broke, or it needed to be removed for cleaning. So I made two straps in the sand colors and sewed velcro on as a closure. When looking through the back of the piece, the sandy straps help to strengthen the illusion that you are looking at an aquarium through glass. I also love the way the imperfections in the glass help imply water movement as you turn your head or change your angle of view.

In all, I would have to say that this piece was truly a challenge, and the results of some of my decisions surprised even me. For example, when I decided on the colors for the fish, I didn't think too much about how the color of the background beads would affect the colors of the fish. I was delighted with the mysterious look the fish took on when I placed the brick in my bay window. It reminded me of a long-ago trip to Hawaii in which my brother and I went scuba diving. Everything under the water had the same sort of blue-green hue that the fish in the Challenge piece took on when light passed through them, and the deeper we went, the more shadowy the fish looked.

I had a huge project bag which I took everywhere with me so that I could work on the project whenever I had a free moment. I received a lot of attention when I pulled out the partly finished peyote cover, which did not yet have any embellishments. One of the most frequently asked questions was, "Where did you find the cloth for that?" Some of them even asked that question after reaching out and feeling the beads! It was interesting to see the expressions on their faces after I explained and they realized that the entire background was just beads—most people thought that I was sewing the beads to a piece of cloth that was the same color as the beads! One of the reasons I love peyote—it really has the look and feel of cloth.

Danielle Embry

I am currently pursuing a fine arts degree through the University of Arizona. I tend toward beadwork for my own artistic expression. There's something extremely satisfying and meditative about the process, not to mention the sheer beauty that beads have to offer to a work of art.

I took a non-credit class in working with seed beads about nine years ago, and I have been a self-proclaimed "bead freak" ever since. It changed the course of my art, and I began to think about my sketches in terms of beads, determining how they would look next to each other, and how the light would play off of them. When I'm doing beaded embroidery, I love the wonderful textural differences you can achieve by using different shapes and sizes. I work in Tucson as a self-employed jeweler, a job which evolved from my initial passion for beads. I made beaded earrings, bracelets, and amulet purses first, and later learned how to work with silver and gemstones. In the future, I would like to incorporate my metalwork into some of my beaded pieces. This wall hanging, *Mermaids*, is composed completely in the brick stitch. I actually hadn't used Delica beads before, but I had read about how well they lend themselves to this weave because of their uniformity. I have a lot of drawing experience and I wanted to experiment with drawing figures in beads. I've made a number of amulet purses, and I always loved the design potential of the brick weave. In the past I tended to use geometric or ethnic patterns and designs, so I thought it might be fun to take it a little farther. I've found the fluid lines of Art Noveau style inspirational for many years, especially the drawings of Mucha. I think that Art Noveau has a very "liquid" quality, and the mermaids were inspired by this type of design. I proceeded to create the pattern with my computer. I downloaded a beading program off the Internet which allowed me to take a design I had scanned in, and place that design behind a graph. I could then follow the lines easily and change colors quickly to suit my drawing.

Bernadette Trahan *Judge's Choice*

I have always been creative and I'm always in the midst of at least three projects. I haven't had any artistic training nor have I attended any beading classes; instead I have learned beading from books and magazines. I also deal in vintage jewelry and accessories, so I've had a lot of hands-on experience repairing old beaded bags. By taking them apart and repairing the beadwork and fringe, I found I really enjoyed the minute detail and even the tediousness of beading. I'm always finding beautiful components, such as the cameo in this piece, in jewelry that has long since come apart. I like to incorporate something old into all of my beadwork.

The antique shell cameo was my inspiration for *Neptune's Garden*. For additional ideas I gathered real seashells and used a book on seashells as a reference. The cameo hangs from a branch of real

Alaskan gem coral and is surrounded by brick stitch and branched fringe, forming the "coral" frame. The shells, starfish, and seaweed are combinations of brick and peyote stitches which I attached to a supporting base strip of peyote. The old hook and eye clasp hides beneath a real seashell framed in brick stitch. My name in gold-filled wire was the finishing touch.

This is the only contest I've ever entered, so it's been very exciting. So far my beadwork pieces are in my own collection or given as gifts. One day I hope to take my hobby further but until then I'm looking forward to the next Delica Challenge!

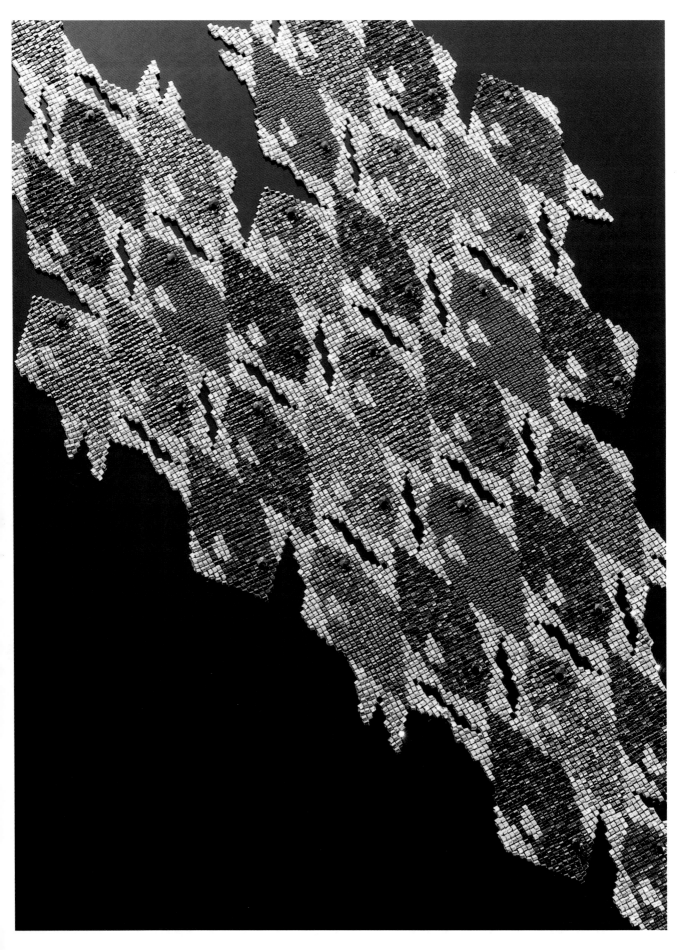

Donald Pierce *2nd Prize*

I became a bead loom artisan on Saturday afternoon January 24, 1987, when I wandered into an exhibit of beadwork called The Bead Goes On which was on display at the Maude Kerns Art Center in Eugene, Oregon. I was so impressed that I returned one hundred miles in a driving rainstorm the next day. In particular, the work of Virginia Blakelock was my downfall.

I am self-taught, with the help of Blakelock's book, ***Those Bad Bad Beads***. I have strived to expand the methodology of loom beading and to achieve a variety of effects.

I currently teach loom beading all around the country. My workshops emphasize design and structure, introducing students to a wide variety of ideas and techniques.

I based this piece on a quilt design, and chose it for the subject matter and the degree of difficulty. It was woven on an 8"x 38" bead loom using Nymo size A thread. Leaving many tails, etc. on the outside of the piece along with the voids within the piece increased the degree of difficulty by a factor of four or five. The technique used in creating the negative spaces was either the interrupted warp/supplemental warp method, or the pull and pray method. The antique nailhead beads in four colors were appliqued after the balance of the piece was completed.

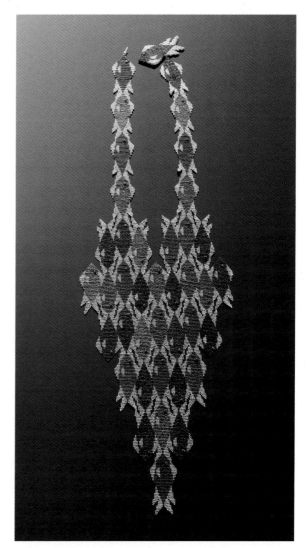

Donald Pierce's creations have appeared extensively in galleries and group shows. For more information about his work, see Alice Scherer's article, "A Sensual Appreciation," in the Summer 1995 issue of Ornament.

Ann Evans Gilbert

As a child, I loved to string beads. After my move from San Francisco to the East Coast, my desire to bead lay dormant for many years only to be reignited in 1995 when I participated in a two-drop peyote bracelet class. The samples of beaded bags on display in the class caught my attention. What were they but small containers? Having studied basketry for years with many nationally and internationally known teachers, all of a sudden beading was justified as an extension of my basketry. I was, after all, already using beads in many of my basket necklaces, which featured tiny woven baskets with beads hanging from the ends of the straps on either side of the basket.

Predominantly a self-taught bead artist, I began to analyze stitch patterns and realized that there were many beadwork techniques that could be improved by incorporating a few minor changes. I began to make beaded amulet bags using Delica beads. With the many colors that are available, my work has taken on a "painting with beads" perspective.

For the Challenge entry, I decided to make a beaded bag. After choosing loom work for its speed and ease of design, many hours were spent at the computer graphing, arranging and rearranging the design. This was followed by more hours looking for just the right colors of Delica beads to portray the design. Not an easy task when working from color cards. The next phase was to construct a loom that would sit upright on a work surface and that was large enough to accommodate the design. Then: beading, beading, beading!

My completed entry, *Seascape*, evolved into a reversible beaded amulet purse that depicts five different types of tropical fish as they swim through three types of plant life. The piece was finished using a combination of square stitch, edging, overlay stitch, and branched fringe.

The materials in the entry included twenty-five colors of Delica beads with oxblood coral and miscellaneous shells for the embellishment. Thread of choice was Silamide in off-white and light brown. For the lining I selected an off-white silk so as not to change the appearance of any of the many bead colors. In completing the entry, I intentionally included imperfect shells and beads to represent the sands of time: the combined impact of tides and humanity.

Ann Evans Gilbert currently teaches both basketry and beadwork. She spends her time designing, graphing, and publishing patterns, marketing patterns and kits, preparing class proposals, completing custom pieces, teaching classes, and operating a small bead shop out of her home. She is also the founder and first president of the new Nebraska Bead Society. Ann is currently working on an instructional/design book of beaded amulet bags that will incorporate several beading techniques and a design theme that targets "painting with beads."

Paula Adams *Judge's Choice*

Although I have had no formal training in art, I own my own graphic-art business. I started beading in 1990 after receiving a pair of earrings created using the brick stitch. I received the earrings on Thursday and by Monday I had figured out how to make them and had fifteen pairs. I am primarily self-taught; however, I have taken a couple of classes from some other fine beaders here in Albuquerque. Over the last seven years my love for beading has not diminished at all. I still love creating beautiful pieces of art and developing new techniques. I have been teaching advanced beading classes for over six years at my favorite store in Albuquerque, Arts & Crafts Mart. My students are a constant challenge to me, always wanting more classes.

My entry, *Music by the Sea*, was created using the flat peyote stitch. Increases and decreases with a little hidden support gave the piece its three dimensional look. The inside was created using the branch stitch on a flat peyote base. The base of the music box was created using peyote in the round, with branch stitch as the accent. I had already been planning to create an oyster incorporating some of my three dimensional work, so when I heard about the Challenge I knew what I wanted to do. However, I did not plan on the time involved—over two hundred hours!

Susan C. Thomas

As an art teacher I've experimented with a large variety of media and techniques. For many years I was very interested in origami. I received a grant in 1991 that enabled me to study origami for two weeks in Japan. I see a definite connection between the perfection in folding which I sought in origami and my approach to beading.

I became serious about beading when I took a workshop at an Art Education Association of Indiana conference on bead embroidery from Terri Brown, owner of Just Beads in Indianapolis and an expert beader. I created a series of embroidered pins with leather backs. My designs from the beginning have always been originals. Once I was confident with the technique, I taught it for two years to eighth graders with impressive results.

For the past two years I've been interested in creating amulet purses. The initial problem was finding Delica beads. I asked a local store on the Purdue campus to carry a line of Delicas. The owner agreed if I could generate some interest to make it worth the purchase. An employee and I organized a workshop that I taught and the owner has carried Delicas and other beads ever since. I have made around thirty-five amulet purses, taught peyote stitch to eighth graders (those willing to stay after school), as well as giving workshops at a local high school.

I actually began my entry three times. My first two attempts were not interesting or fun enough. Finally I saw a comical pair of bikini earrings which inspired my entry, *Picnic at the Beach (Bikini Packed Within)*. I used tubular peyote stitch for the body of the bag and flat peyote for the necklace. I like the Art Deco style of my former works and that's why I chose a simple striped beach towel for the front. The sunglasses seemed like the icon that would subtly draw attention to the fact that they were sitting on a beach towel. I graphed the sunglasses beforehand to make sure they forced the towel to lay horizontally. The contrasting design of the picnic table cloth on the other side of the bag is done in the colors of a beautiful seashell that I bought. I felt the colors sparkled like sand in bright light. Finally, I felt that the hidden bikini, revealed by sliding the top of the bag up the strap, was a funny surprise.

Susan C. Thomas holds BA and MA degrees in art education. She has taught art for almost thirteen years, mostly at the middle school level.

Margaret Ball

I've done fiber arts of one sort or another most of my life—embroidery, weaving, quilting, surface design, and now, beadwork—all self-taught. *The Merrow*, like most of my other pieces, probably shows that I'm coming from a background of fabric manipulation rather than pure beadwork. It's a seated mermaid about nine inches high. Merrow is an Anglo-Irish word for mermaid. I first sketched this piece within view of the Irish Sea so it seemed an appropriate title.

The basic form of *The Merrow* is constructed of a wire armature wrapped with batting and covered with blue silk. The silk was then completely covered with Delica beads and machine-made lace (constructed using iridescent threads and scraps of organza on a water-soluble base). The lace and seed beads were then partially covered in some areas by a second layer of netting in Delicas. Where the netting hangs free from the arms, back of the head, and tail, larger glass beads are used at the crossing points and to weight the fringe. A scattering of mother-of-pearl charms and glass beads adorns the tail, trapped between the basic layer of lace and beads and the upper layer of netting. The beadwork over the breast is extended with free peyote stitch to give the effect of white foam on the waves. The face is an irregular oval of paua shell, held in place by glue and seed bead stitching around the edges.

Besides figural pieces, I make small quilts, generally combining photo transfers with heavy bead embellishment. I play with images in Adobe Photoshop, print them either onto transfer paper or directly onto fabric, put them together into mini-quilts, and embellish the surface with beads.

I started beading a couple of years ago, and didn't start entering pieces in competitions until this spring. No awards, but I've had some pictures published in the "Your Work" section of <u>Bead and Button</u> and had two pieces juried into the Embellishment '97 show, one of which they kept for display at the Houston Quilt Show.

I've had one workshop with Mimi Holmes and another with Donna Milliron; the second inspired me to get a kiln and start fusing glass. When I have more control of this medium I hope to add larger pendants and glass masks to the beaded figures I've been making.

I belong to the Austin Bead Society, but usually don't make it to meetings. (The meetings are at night, and have an uncanny way of coinciding with Back-to-School Night or basketball practice or one of the other activities that clutter the lives of parents.) I'm on a beaders' Internet mailing list and get a lot of input and inspiration from the messages there as well as from the pictures people have posted on the Web.

The images and ideas for my work are probably closely linked to my "real" work, which is writing fantasy and science fiction novels. You would EXPECT a science fiction writer to come up with images of drowned cities, and women turning into trees, wouldn't you?

Margaret's next book, co-authored with Anne McCaffrey, is titled **Acorna's Quest**. *It will be published by Harper-Collins.*

CarolAnne Bouchles

Being creative has always been part of who I am. My poor mother had to deal with it ever since I was young, when I decided to paint a design on the hardwood floor with green food coloring! I have explored and experimented with all types of media. In school I took all the art and graphics classes that I could.

Years ago, I was in a craft store and walked down the aisle of beads. Curious, I picked up a book and thumbed through it. When I first saw seed beads I said to myself, "No way! These are way too small." Well, that thought didn't last too long and soon I was beading up a storm. Finally I looked in the mirror and confessed to myself, "I am a bead-a-holic." My library of beading books and my ever-growing inventory of beads were the true evidence.

I started a home-based jewelry business which allowed me to be as creative as I wanted and also to get paid for what I loved doing most. Being a self-taught beader, most of my jewelry was a learn-as-you-go kind of thing. The finished pieces were their own reward. Beading has always come easy for me. I enjoy off-loom beading the most. My specialties are peyote, brick, and loom work. I love to see my designs come to life as every bead is added on.

When I decided to enter the 1st Miyuki Delica Challenge, I wanted to do something that would capture the essence of my home state of Maine. That is why I chose to do a lobster. I call my entry *Entangled in Sea Beads*. I included textured seaweed and twisted fringe to represent the rolling Maine coast. I used tubular brick stitch to bead the base of the amulet bag and freeform brick stitch for the claws and the tail. The bottom of the bag is embellished with twisted fringe.

CarolAnne has published a number of amulet purse patterns. She can be contacted at MadCatBead@aol.com.

Suzanne Cooper

My most important beading class was the first one I took. Three years ago in Santa Fe I fell in love with amulet purses and wanted so badly to learn to beadweave. The bead store was closing in forty-five minutes when I met a delightful teenager named Sierra who was an excellent beadweaver. I offered to pay her for a quick private lesson and in that short time she got me off to a great start.

Since then my involvement with beads has taken over my life! I have published two books on amulet purses and have a new book on evening purses in the final stages of completion. It seems that all my training in the various art fields was preparing me for beadwork. The color and design theory of painting classes, the sculptural aspects of jewelry making and all my studies of stained glass have come together in these tiny, magical orbs of colored glass!

I decided to make my little sunken treasure chest after watching a documentary about the discovery of a ship that sank many years ago off the Florida coast. Ahhhh, the romance of finding lost treasure!

I titled my entry *Pilfering the Pirate's Plunder*. The chest was covered with white doeskin and the entire outside was covered with beads woven in the peyote stitch. The sand was made with a combination of peyote stitch and free-form lazy stitch to depict the irregular surface of the ocean floor. Small seashells were drilled and woven into the piece. Jewels, coins and other objects were affixed in place using E-6000 adhesive. The body of the octopus was woven in peyote stitch over a round ball of styrofoam and the legs were done in peyote stitch with a surface embellishment on both sides. Seaweeds were done in free-form peyote stitch. The coral combines peyote stitch with surface embellishment and branched fringe and includes small pieces of real coral woven into the beads.

*Prior to becoming a bead addict, Suzanne Cooper's artistic ventures included studying oil painting and jewelry design and fabrication in both gold and silver at San Antonio College. Her exploration of stained glass includes fifteen years of studying with leading artists in the fused glass field. She has written over twenty-one design books for stained glass and has taught and lectured nationwide. Her bead training includes classes with Don Pierce in split loom weaving, work with David Chatt, and a master class in peyote from Barbara Grainger. She belongs to the San Antonio Bead and Ornament Society. Her two books on amulet purses are **Dancing Light** and **Uniquely Yours**. More beading books are in progress.*

My shell purse, *Sea-N-Things*, began with the idea of a scallop shell. I then expanded that idea to include many of the aquatic forms I see when I scuba dive on the Laguna reefs in California. I stitched the "petals" of the shell first, then filled in the gaps with peyote stitch. The back was done the same way. The two sides were stitched together near the edge which left a shallow pocket on each side. I filled that with branched fringe and then added embellishments.

Suzanne Wester

Grandmother Humboldt is a beaded loom weaving using Miyuki 11/0 Delicas. It contains seventeen thousand six hundred beads in twenty-six colors. *Grandmother Humboldt* represents a Native American shaman woman named after the Humboldt Current located off the west coast of the Americas.

She rises out of the sea as a blue wave sprinkled with phosphorescent foam. The "eye" on her cape and the black curve from her head into the crest of the wave is a reference to the sea eagle totems of the Kwakiutl Indians. Look closely and you can see the eye and beak of the sea eagle emerge. The shape of her garb and earrings are Nakoaktok, another Native American Indian tribe from the Pacific Northwest.

Her eyes are created as optical illusions. View her closely and you will see a woman in a meditative pose with her eyes closed. This peacefulness symbolizes the calmness, harmony, and beauty the sea can possess.

Blink and look at her again and you will see a woman with a wild and terrifying stare of horrifying proportions. Her piercing blue eyes will pull you into the beaded painting even as you try to escape. This wildness symbolizes the tempestuous nature of the sea and the dreadful terrors lurking in the deep.

Neva Wuerfel *1st Prize*

I began beading six or seven years ago. As most addictions begin slowly, my taste for beads was initially moderate. Those were the days when I designed a specific item, then bought just enough beads to complete it. The beads worked their way into my life, though, and soon I needed to buy this one or that one simply because it was beautiful. I figured a project would come along to justify the purchase. Soon, the complexity of my designs required larger quantities of beads. Certainly it saved money and time to buy full strands rather than counting out enough single beads for a project. After all, who could tell how many would be needed?

When a job opportunity brought our family to New Mexico in January 1996, I knew I was in the right place to further my beadwork. I had already been working in the peyote stitch and looked for a place in Albuquerque to purchase the seed beads I needed. I found a shop which offered classes in numerous techniques. I was surprised to find one of the instructors was Margo Fields, an artist published in *The Amulet Purse*, a book that I refer to faithfully. I signed up for classes at once, and it has been a joy to learn from such a talented seed bead artist! I convinced my husband we needed a trip to Tucson for the February 1996 bead shows. We spent all of Saturday at the two shows and could not believe the amazing pieces people were making with beads. Jim, until this point unaffected, was taken by the desire to make glass beads. We were like groupies, talking with the artists and

asking them to autograph the show poster. All the way home we talked about how much fun it would be to try this as a hobby.

Over the next year, we decided to follow our dream. We purchased tools and supplies and worked hard to improve our techniques and skills. In fact, the cost was so great that we made a pact to sell enough to earn back our initial investment. We felt a need to justify our obsession. That's how it happened, a natural progression over time which has led me to choose beads as a permanent part of my personal and professional life.

Initially, I wanted to work with haiku or another literary source as my inspiration. I thought a Japanese sea theme would have been suitable, but after trips to the library and bookstore did not inspire workable ideas, I began looking through books with sea animals. I then encountered a new obstacle: the shipping box parameters of 18" x 18" x 6". Many subjects seemed to work out in an overall cubical format, scaling the work down to about 6" x 6" x 6". I wanted to work on a larger scale. The search began for a creature with broad width and compact height to fill that oddly-shaped box.

I found the perfect circular shape of a plankton, *Porpita pacifico*, in a coral reef book. The book offered a top view only. I interpreted the profile view from photos of jellyfish, while considering structural and display issues. I worked directly from the photo, breaking it down into basic shapes that I could reproduce in beadwork. The photo also inspired the color palette. I was especially taken with the visual impact of the radiating spokes. At first, I planned to make more than one hundred spokes, but thankfully this was not necessary to fill the form. If I had known how many monotonous hours would be spent making these, I might never have begun. In the end, I needed only fifty-seven to achieve the fullness I desired. I could not have done many more. The rest of the work was very pleasurable, and seemed expeditious in comparison.

The beaded disk shapes were executed in peyote stitch. The large disk is worked in two-drop peyote stitch with standard and 8/0 Delicas. I worked the top disk in single peyote stitch, with added surface embellishment. As the crowning finish, I commissioned my husband to lampwork the finial, which allows easy removal of the top disk for access to the lamp bulb. I chose fishing monofilament as my stringing material to maintain the translucency of the Delicas. Initially, I wanted the spokes covered with peyote stitch to give a very straight edge to the beadwork at the termination of each rod. After working several samples, I realized I did not like the zig-zag relationship of the beads; I wanted a smoother flow. I chose to string the beads, including the spikes until I had several feet. I wrapped the strands in a spiral fashion around the acrylic rod, adjusting the spikes as I went along, then used hypo-tube cement to adhere. I repeated these steps until each rod was covered. At this point, each rod was organized by size, distributed around the circumference of the large tube, then glued into place.

The inspiration to wire the sculpture as a light fixture came late in the design process. I've always been interested in light fixtures as a subject, and the translucency of my entry, *Porpita Pacifico*, encouraged the additional effort. During the first fitting of the spokes, I was thrilled to see a glow radiate down each one, exactly as I had envisioned.

My involvement with quilting, which dates back over ten years, is what got me started with beading. About two years ago I was attending a quilt show in Williamsburg, Virginia, with a friend when we saw an advertisement for a local bead shop and decided to find it. Once through the front door, I was mesmerized by the variety of beads. Having no idea where to begin in the selection process, I simply filled a tray with what caught my eye. An hour and a half later I walked out with thirty-five dollars worth of beads. Considering my comment as we left the store, that "I would never work with those little things," the rest is history.

After seeing the show The Beaded Object in Asheville, North Carolina, I got the incentive to tackle the 1st Miyuki Delica Challenge. The theme given for the competition inspired numerous possibilities. I listed ideas and struck the ones I thought would be too ordinary. I had always wanted to bead a tin can. Every trip to the supermarket, I would scrutinize all the shelves containing tin cans, looking for the unusual. I knew the tuna can related to the sea but that just wasn't enough. I felt I had to develop the idea a bit more. I could place a mermaid in the can, but that would be too commonplace. Finally I remembered the Charlie® Tuna commercials and developed the idea with him in mind.

Here is a summary of the techniques I used:
- Single peyote stitch over the tuna can
- Free form peyote stitch, branched fringe, and surface embellishments with assorted glass beads for the sculpted Charlie® Tuna
- Brick stitch for the Sorry Charlie® sign
- Circular peyote stitch and netting for the inner can lid.

Sorry Charlie almost didn't see the light of day. I started beading my entry in March, and finished in July, 1997. During those months my life was turned upside down and inside out due to personal illness and my mother being involved in a serious car accident from which she is still rehabilitating. Many beads, hundreds of hours later, and with the encouragement of my husband and children I completed *Sorry Charlie*.

STAR-KIST, CHARLIE and SORRY CHARLIE are registered trademarks of Star-Kist Foods, Inc.

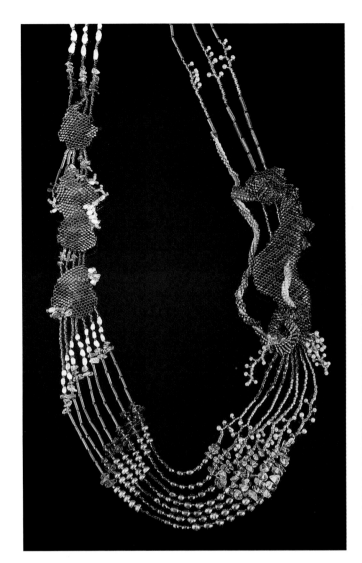

Margo Field

I have been a pharmacist for twenty years but have always had a need for some sort of artistic outlet. Over the years I have sewn, done various types of needle crafts, and played with pastels and oils—always looking for the right medium that would light my pathway to creative expression. Six years ago I discovered beads. Now my pathway is a super highway!

There is a wonderful shop in Albuquerque called Arts & Crafts Mart owned by Jackie Fallis. She taught me basic beadwork techniques and gave me wonderful encouragement and support to pursue my "bead dreams." She also made it possible for me to teach classes using my own designs.

I have been teaching intermediate to advanced classes for four years. Two years ago I opened Poppy Field Bead Company which is a bead store next to Arts & Crafts Mart. The two stores have a symbiotic relationship which is much like having two great bead stores at one location.

My philosophy about beading is: do it for *fun*! Explore color, form, and texture. But more important, explore your own self. What seems so amazing to me is that while beading in itself may appear to be a rather solitary pursuit, one can meet and "connect" with so many others. I thoroughly enjoy teaching beadwork to others and relish the camaraderie of operating a bead store.

Let me add that I do very little tangible planning before starting a piece. I do a *lot* of thinking about it, but when I sit down I want to work with beads, not paper and pencil or computer. Before doing this sea horse I had done a three dimensional hummingbird. One of my friends suggested a sea horse, but I thought it would be too difficult. She said that if I could do a hummingbird I surely could do a sea horse. I didn't want to disappoint her!

My entry, *FantaSea*, features the sea horse—an unusual creature of the sea of such imagination and poetry of form that one could almost believe it is a fantasy. The asymmetrical work places the sea horse among nautical plants and balances him with waves and surf. The clasp represents a starfish.

The sea horse and waves are done in peyote stitch. The strand of seaweed that is entwined by the creature's tail is a type of twisted beadwork that I discovered by serendipity. The shape of the sea horse comes entirely from stitching together the Delicas. It has not been stuffed, wired or supported by any foundation.

Materials used are: Miyuki Delicas, freshwater pearls, blue topaz, iolite and peridot chips, old coral beads, old Japanese glass pearls (2mm), vintage and contemporary glass bugle beads, sterling wire and Nymo thread.

Margo Field won Third Place in the seed bead category at the first Embellishment International Bead and Button Show in Austin, Texas in 1995 and Best of Show in the Fiber Arts Fiesta at Albuquerque in 1997 in the New Mexico Bead Society Competition. One of her early pieces, Queen Isabella, *is featured in the gallery of **Beaded Amulet Purses** by Nicolette Stessin and many of her creations appear in Peggy Sue Henry's **Beads to Buckskins** series volumes 9 and 12. She belongs to the New Mexico Bead Society.*

Lynn Smythe

I have a Bachelor of Arts degree in geology from the University of Rochester in Rochester, New York, and have taken classes in fashion merchandising. Previously, I worked as a manager for So-Fro Fabrics in New York and Connecticut. I recently completed a four-week casting class (lost wax method) taught by Bill Flora, a member of the gem and mineral society I belong to.

I began beading three years ago, while looking for a hobby to occupy my free time. What started out as a hobby quickly turned into a full-time obsession. I had to have bracelets to match the beaded earrings and necklaces to match the bracelets.

I teach beading classes through a local bead store, and to members of my gem and mineral society. I won third prize in the jewelry category at the 1996 and 1997 Havana Bead Festival in Florida.

I have an affinity for dolphins. I have a dolphin tattoo on my right shoulder and call my business Dolphin Crafts. I wanted to incorporate dolphins in the design for my personal amulet bag.

Twilight Ocean Dancers was done in flat peyote stitch using twelve shades of Miyuki Delicas. The side fringe and neckstrap use various beads (seed, glass, freshwater pearls) to invoke the feeling of an underwater reef scene.

I also created four one-of-a-kind beaded beads which are incorporated into the neckstrap. The beads are tubular peyote stitch around either a wood or plastic core bead with three dimensional surface embellishment using Delicas, 14/0 seed beads, and Miyuki drop beads. Each beaded bead took two to three hours to create.

Lynn is a member of the Gem and Mineral Society of the Palm Beaches which meets in West Palm Beach, Florida. In addition she edits the newsletter and manages the website <http://members.aol.com/dlphcrft/society.htm> for the Treasure Coast Bead Society which meets in Port St. Lucie, Florida. She plans to form the Palm Beach Bead Society which will be based in Delray Beach, Florida.

She also operates a small retail mail order business, Dolphin Crafts, which offers beads, books, and supplies; sells her beadwork through five galleries and at local art shows; and has had three articles on beading published with a fourth article pending.

1. "A Lovely, Lacy Miniature Pouch"; May/June 1997 issue of <u>Jewelry Crafts</u>; pages 12-15.
2. "Bead-Netted Cabochon"; September 1997 issue of <u>Lapidary Journal</u>; pages 79-81.
3. "Beaded Comanche Rosettes"; November/December 1997 issue of <u>Jewelry Crafts</u>; pages 52-55, 59.
4. "Quick and Easy Macrame Earrings"; pending publication in <u>Lapidary Journal</u>.

Jacqué Owens

I started beading about six years ago. I was going on vacation and needed something to work on that didn't require a lot of space. So I took a small loom that my daughter had abandoned when she discovered boys. That small loom created a monster! My grandson calls it the bead bug. My husband says he is now a bead widower and a patron of the arts because of the money he has invested in beads.

Shortly after I started beading, I noticed a small dark spot on the top of my hand. When I was finally diagnosed with scleroderma, the doctors told me I might lose the use of my right hand. I continued to bead thinking I might not be able to for much longer. The beadwork proved to be therapeutic. My scleroderma is now in remission so I guess I will bead forever. Although beading started as a hobby, it eventually led me to do my first show. A couple of years later my daughter began to bead with me. Now we teach together and do several shows a year. The only class I have taken was at the 1997 Austin Embellishment show. It was a beaded mask class taught by NanC Meinhardt.

The technique used for the kimono, *The Sea*, was circular peyote for the body and sleeves. I used flat peyote for the tops of the kimono and sleeves and brick stitch for the white around the edges.

My entry was inspired by an article in the <u>Smithsonian</u> magazine. The article was about a Japanese artist who makes hand-crafted, tie-dyed kimonos; his art is called Tsujigahana. The colors of his kimonos reminded me of Delica beads, so I decided to make a kimono for the contest.

Jacqué teaches at Beadazzles in Atlanta, Georgia, Bama Beads in Tuscaloosa, Alabama, and soon at the Chevron Trading Post in Asheville, North Carolina. She also sells Delica beads and teaches out of her home. She is currently the president of the Atlanta Bead Society.

Emlee Young

My love of beads started when I was a small child. I was fascinated with a small beaded bouquet of my grandmother's. When she passed on the flowers were given to a cousin and I was heartbroken. Later, as an adult, I decided to make a bouquet for myself. I had no instructions and made the flowers as I remembered them. That was the start of my bead collection and my love of beading.

After studying many instruction books, I have found that I like combining techniques and making my own patterns. I also like to combine media. Recently I made a stained glass lamp with beaded insets. Dolls are a love of mine and I have made beaded clothes for them. I have taught beading one-on-one, but now I am planning to teach at the "Bead Weavers," an offshoot of "The Yarn Winders," our local weavers' guild here in Marquette, Michigan.

After raising my four children I went back to school. I earned an associates degree in costuming and a bachelor's degree in theater at Northern Michigan University. I do costuming from my home and design for the area community theater.

As you can see, my life is full of creative endeavors. I love it and thank God for my talent.

The Mermaid was inspired from the natural shell form of the bodice. I strung the pale green rayon thread with sea-green and pearl colored Delica beads. Then I crocheted the body, dropping or adding stitches as needed to give it shape. The tail fin is done with an elaborated peyote stitch. I very carefully drilled holes in the shell to attach the bodice and again used an ornate peyote or gourd stitch. The necklace cord is twisted thread with pre-strung beads.

Caravan Beads

Jane Warnick

I've had years of studying art and design in workshops and seminars across the country. I studied color and design with Constance Howard, Barbara Lee Smith, Wilke Smith, Pat Lambert, and others. I also studied fabric design and belonged to a fiber arts design group for many years. My college years were spent studying English literature and philosophy, so I had a lot of catching up to do.

When did I start beading? Does crocheting ropes of pearls in the 1960s count? I'd say I've dabbled in beading for at least the last ten years, and took it up seriously about three years ago. I have studied with Carol Wilcox Wells, Kate Drew Wilkinson, and Therese Spears. My background is in the fiber arts: machine and hand embroidery, canvaswork, quilting, and wearable art. I lectured and taught in all those disciplines in the 1970s and 1980s. During those years I also wrote columns, book reviews, and articles for various magazines, and coauthored (with Jackie Dodson) two books, Chilton's *Know Your Brother Sewing Machine* and *Gifts Galore*.

I used peyote stitch to weave my entry, *She Sells Sea Shells*. The neckpiece is constructed with the spiral rope technique featured on the Hillsinger Country website <http://rogue.northwest.com/~ahwaley>. The fringe is simply beads strung on thread.

Deciding what to make was the hardest part of the competition. I thought of all the things about the sea which I love: tide pools teeming with color, rocks tumbled to a smooth perfection, seashells of every color and shape, the regular pounding of waves. I designed a freeform necklace incorporating slices of shells. I began beading it and realized that it simply wasn't me. My designs have always been based on regular patterns, tessellations, repeats. So I went to the computer to design the overall seashell pattern composed of a spiral and a clam shell shape. I set the shells against a graduated background of blue, going from the darkest at the bottom to the lightest at the top. I constructed the neckpiece in the spiral rope to reinforce the spiral of the larger shell shapes and to introduce tiny beads like seafoam bubbles. The fringe was added to represent the movement and sound of water. I reversed the gradation in the fringe, beginning with the darkest blue, taking it to the lightest, and ending with an almost clear blue topaz. I added a bit of fringe in the shell colors to the bottom of the bag and wound a thread of beads and pearls through the neckpiece to integrate the rusty peaches with the blues.

Ingrid Gilbert

As a self-taught artist, I have explored a number of media (paint, sculpture, fiber, and others). At this stage of my life, one of my goals is to make use of as many of the skills that I've learned as possible in each piece of artwork.

Over the years I've watched my art library change from post-impressionist masters to Paleolithic and aboriginal artwork. The seed from which art as we know it has grown is the basic human need to express the divine; that truth is my starting point.

More specifically, when I began this particular piece I had been thinking about creating a series of goddess icons based loosely on old Paleolithic figures. I also wanted to bring something new to the endeavor. I had recently been looking at Tibetan ritual tools such as the "djore" and "phurba knife." The djore is used to balance energy, the knife to cut through illusion. The tools are invested with symbols indicative of their use. I found this concept very interesting, so I created the piece to be looked at as artwork, but also as a ritual tool to be held in the hand and used to draw or focus energy. I hope to make my figures transcend the bounds of any particular religious philosophy. They are meant to be used according to the need and inspiration of the owner.

The techniques I used were circular and flat peyote stitch over an original clay sculpture incorporating a quartz crystal and boulder opal. Embellishments are coral, pearl, shell, turquoise, and blue topaz.

Pregnant Sea Goddess is part of an ongoing series.

Jill D'Allesandro

I began making and selling beaded jewelry to small stores when I was in college. Since then I have continued to bead, exploring the realm of small sculpture. I approach a beaded sculpture in a similar way to a sculpture made of stiffened cloth or paper. I start by creating a frame, then use peyote stitch to make a beaded cloth to fit the contours of the frame. Peyote stitch is my favorite beading technique because it is so versatile. By adding or decreasing beads I am able to control the form. I have found Delicas to be extremely well-suited to bead sculpture. Their flat edges enable them to fit closely together creating a rigid, self-supporting form.

To make *Mussel Shells*, I began by threading beads on thin wire. Then I simply filled in the interior using peyote stitch, increasing or decreasing to fit the contours of the shell. I did not follow a pattern, preferring to work free-form from shells I collected on the beach.

I consider *Mussel Shells* to be realistic beadwork. The shores of the Maine coast are covered with rocks, seaweed, and mussel shells. In recreating these shells, I strove not only to capture a likeness but also to glorify the abundance of Maine's oceanic resources.

Jill D'Alessandro received her Bachelor of Fine Arts degree (with a concentration in fibers) from Scripps College, Claremont, California, in 1990. She is presently a second year graduate student in the Fibers Department at the Tyler School of Art in Philadelphia. She has participated in numerous art exhibits during the past decade.

Jessica Fitzgerrel *Judge's Choice*

As a kid I always enjoyed drawing, making sculptures, and sewing. I was a 4-H member for seven years, most often doing crafts. In high school I spent a lot of time in art classes. I went on to get a degree in visual arts in college. I didn't have any interest in beads until about six years ago when African beads, Fimo beads, Czech glass, charms, and other beads were being sold in a store where I worked. That's when I became addicted! I began buying beads that caught my eye, not thinking of making anything. Eventually I ended up with three of one kind and five or six of another kind of bead and hanks of colors that didn't match, and I didn't even know which kind of threads or sizes of needles to use to sew them together. The more popular beading became, however, the easier it got to find information and supplies. My creativity expanded as my collection got bigger.

Eventually I learned peyote stitch so I could make an amulet bag. At the time I was using "tile" beads which I later learned were Delicas. After that the challenge was to discover what else I could make with peyote stitch. I just kept getting more ideas out of the stitch and out of each thing I tried.

I used books, magazines, movies, and videos about the sea for inspiration. Finally I decided to create a mask. I had many ideas for the structure of the mask, but in the end I just limited myself to what I had around the house: papier maché, wooden dowels, cheese cloth, paint, and ribbon.

As for the beading, I found some sea stars and shells to use as examples for the ones I beaded on the mask. These were the first three dimensional pieces I had ever made out of beads. I chose the netting because it had the look and feel of nets on boats and was easy to manipulate. The twists, kelp, and more shells were added later.

I didn't really plan my entry, *Morgan*; it just came together through inspiration, trial and error, and how I thought it should look. For me it was truly a learning experience.

Gale Tomlinson *Honorable Mention*

I started beading in July of 1996, taught by a close friend and fellow fashion design classmate. I took one class with Cheri Lyn Waltz which focused on setting a cabochon. I have a significant and well-used beading library which allows me to be pretty much self-taught.

From the beginning I have strived for a broad range of beading. I try to make no two pieces identical. This helps keep my creative interest alive.

I received the guidelines for the Miyuki Delica Challenge from a friend who thought it would be a rewarding thing to do while traveling. Later I found a shell on the Texas seashore. It was simple but beautiful. I thought about Anne Morrow Lindberg's book *Gift from the Sea* as I always do while shelling, and the book and shell became my inspiration. I took the sea shell with me when I chose the Delicas. The shell was mostly gray and rust and lacked energy and pizazz. I began adding various colors. I put them in a separated dish and one by one covered each color only to find that I could not eliminate any of the chosen colors. The combination of the colors was essential to breathing life into the final results.

I started by sketching multiple sizes and configurations until I had one that was good enough to get me started. Then I began searching the library for appropriate stitches and found the two-drop peyote. As I worked, I modified that stitch, not realizing that I was in fact using three- and four-

drop peyote as well. This was necessary to get the desired shape. Later I found that such a stitch had been described and published. I proceeded beading and ripping, beading and ripping (wrong color, wrong shape, etc.) until my entry, Moisson de la Mer, evolved. Once I had completed the basic purse, I embellished it with a second layer of Delicas to achieve the color variations and dimensions I was looking for.

As with much of my work, what I originally saw in my mind was not the finished product; what I sketched was not my final entry piece.

Gale Tomlinson has a degree in fashion design from Harper College, Palatine, Illinois.

Bonnie Bousquet-Smith *Honorable Mention*

I have been interested in color, design, and artistic endeavors ever since I can remember. I have dabbled in many forms including drawing, painting, sculpture, dress designing, and dress making.

In 1989, I took a beadweaving class from Helen Banes through the Washington, D.C. Embroiderers' Guild. That class was the beginning of my professional beading. I had been teaching needlework classes and winning ribbons at local shows (including Woodlawn Plantation) for my needlework. After this class I started combining beadwork with needlework techniques and making jewelry (neckpieces) which I sold. And I began BUYING BEADS!

Ann Benson's book *Beadweaving* came out while I was living in Iceland. That book and her wonderful designs prompted me to look at smaller and smaller beads. When we moved to Maine in 1994, one of the first places I visited was Caravan Beads (whose ad I had seen in <u>Ornament</u> magazine).

A <u>Threads</u> magazine article (September 1994, by Deborah Robson) about how to make amulet purses in Comanche stitch got me started making beaded purses. Soon thereafter I began teaching beading as well. By then I was studying any publication I could find on beads and beading, and exploring and practicing any technique I found. As I became more comfortable, I started combining techniques in purses.

In 1996, it seemed that little neck purses were everywhere. To branch out, I started making small baskets with beads. Then Carol Wilcox Wells' book, *Creative Bead Weaving,* was released. I followed her directions for beaded beads but then I wanted to play more and began making bead faces. I am still excited and stimulated by many ideas in this area.

The techniques I used in making *Neptune's Daughters* were: flat peyote, one-, two- and three-drop peyote, tubular peyote, ruffled peyote, beaded-bead techniques, helix techniques, tubular netting, Ann Benson's beadweaving technique (fins), appliqué (faces), and padded appliqué on the hands. I used right angle weave and patterned right angle weave for the background and tubular right angle weave for the tails. The cord is an eight-bobbin Kumihimo braid which I made to coordinate with the piece.

My idea evolved over the year. I knew I wanted to make a mermaid. At one point I was also going to include Neptune—later, he was only in the name. My actual piece changed when I started looking at some Erté costume designs from the 1920s. His work was monochromatic using bluish greys to muted deep bluish purples. I started with this idea but as I started making the hair for the first mermaid and visualizing her lower body, I decided it would be more fun to do the piece in color combinations: blue, green and purple, while still keeping the basic idea of three mermaids against a backdrop.

The other idea which evolved was which areas would be flat, which would be three dimensional, and how to put these portions together in a way that was both pleasing and visually acceptable.

One of the most fun parts of the planning was deciding which technique could best be employed to create each part of the piece. Right angle weave is so drapey it was perfect for the backdrop and for creating a tail that would twist around other tails. Ann Benson's technique was perfect for making a tail fin that looked like a tail fin.

Suzy Lambert

I have been an avid seamstress for twenty-five years, designing my own clothing as well as clothing for porcelain dolls. In addition, I have sculpted and painted porcelain dolls, studying under doll artist Jacqueline Ball. I have worked with oil and watercolors on canvas and paper respectively. I have been beading for only two years, and find that my experience in other artistic endeavors has helped me in my beadwork. All of my works are original designs. I have had no formal training; I learned my technique by reading books and talking with other bead artists.

The spirit of my amulet purse, *Perpetual Motion,* expresses my belief that life and its environment change continually, yet remain the same in their essence. I used colored pencils on graph paper to design this purse. Tubular peyote stitch was used to create the circular rhythm of the wave. Twisted fringe accented with malachite stones added beauty to the piece. The bottom of the purse is made using flat peyote stitch which include my signature and the date. The strap is made in odd count peyote stitch with a written message including the title of the work. The purse includes fifteen different colors of Delicas.

Kristen Tescher *Honorable Mention*

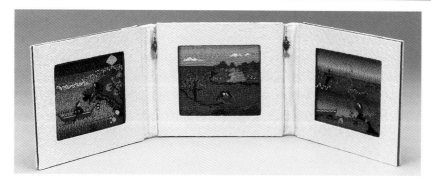

I have been beading since 1992. I prefer the term "self-educated" to "self-taught" because I consider the authors of the books and articles in my bead library to be my teachers. Though I have not had any classes with them, Carol Wilcox Wells, Virginia Blakelock, and Carol Perrenoud are a few of the inspirational artists I've learned from.

My beading studio, The Everything Box, is located in my home in Rockport, Maine. Several of my pieces have been shown by galleries in Maine, and I exhibit my work in juried shows in New England. I am a member of the Maine craft guild Directions, and have also sold my work through Maine Coast Artists.

My husband Nick and I play traditional and Celtic music, and perform and record in Maine. As a musician (I play the harp, guitar, and fiddle), I enjoy using musical themes in much of my beadwork. Many of my amulet bags and earrings have designs of dancers, fiddlers, guitar players, and harpists.

Last year another opportunity for expanding my skills came my way. The owners of a local book bindery, Andrew and Ellen Eddy, had heard that I worked with beads and asked if I would help them with some highly detailed work on a bookbinding project. As I learned techniques of bookbinding, I kept thinking of ways to combine these new skills with beadwork. I had not seen this done before.

My entry, *Beyond the Slope of the Sea,* is my first merging of bookbinding and beadwork. I liked the idea of telling a Japanese story with Japanese beads. I looked through several books of Japanese poetry and loved the story of "The Boy Urashima of Mizunoe." It tells about a young man who goes far out to sea, meets and falls in love with the sea god's daughter, and loses all due to his own foolishness. This poem, by Takahashi Mushimaro, created vivid pictures for me.

I first designed three panels on graph paper, then wove each panel on a bead loom. Other pieces were made with off-loom techniques (brick-stitch, ruffled peyote, and twisted fringe) and stitched to the woven panels. I then used bookbinding techniques to create the fabric frames and hinged unit. I included the narrative with the piece to tell the story.

The project took over two hundred hours to make. It has been tremendously exciting to combine these techniques in a unique way. Currently I am at work on more "bead books" and including texts of stories and songs within the pieces.

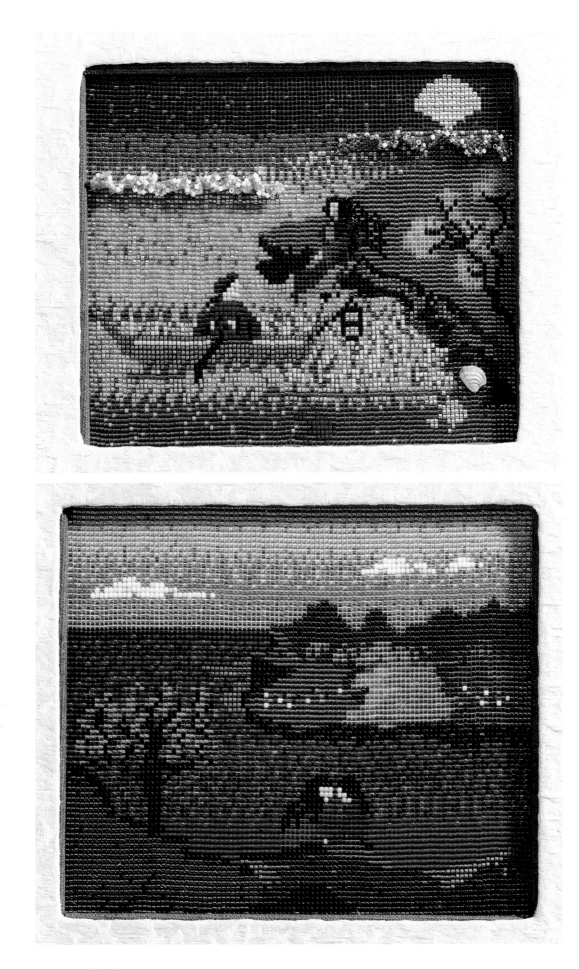

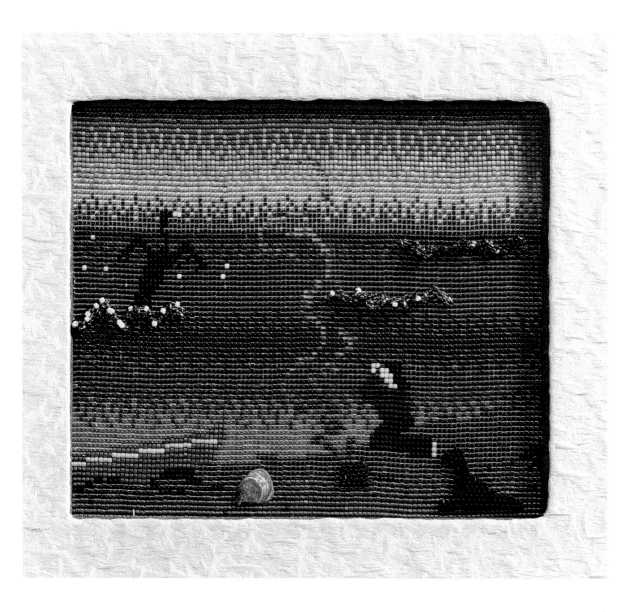

Yoshiko Kitayama

When I heard that the theme of the competition was the sea, I remembered the time when I was a child and went to my parents' home in Shikoku by ferry boat. The fishing fires I saw from the boat were sparkling like jewels. It was very difficult to recreate the dark sea but I hoped to use beads to express the sparkling fires. My tapestry is titled *Fishing Fires*.

Mrs. Kitayama is a director and instructor in the Delica Bead Loom Association of Japan.

Diane Noren

I began beading about four years ago. Teaching myself peyote stitch, I began by making several amulet bags and then found that I could make the human figure in beads. Making three dimensional objects (especially the human figure) is my main focus. I am proficient at peyote stitch, loom weaving, square stitch, brick stitch and Ndebele or herringbone stitch. The base of my piece is loomed and supported by a copper tube that has been stitched in at the top. The bottom was finished with fringe ending in small sea shells. The octopus and moonfish attached to the base are done in peyote stitch. The trigger fish and boxfish attached to the cord are also done in peyote stitch.

I was inspired to make a rainbow trout by a picture in a children's book. When I learned the theme of this contest, I found pictures of saltwater fish that interested me and made them. I then designed the background and attached them to it. I titled my entry *Lots More Fish in the Sea.*

Diane Noren has a bachelor's degree in math with a minor in art. She has been taking classes in both art and crafts since early childhood. In addition to beading, she has designed cloth dolls and published patterns for them. She has also taught at the last four National Cloth Dollmakers Festivals. She currently teaches at Three Beads and a Button in Cupertino, California and will be teaching beading at Wee Folk of Cloth in Baltimore, Maryland in October of 1998. She is a member of the South Bay Seed Bead Guild.

Kathy Rice

The very first beadwork I did was in the early 1970s. I did a few chains, made a few necklaces and earrings, but that was it. I rediscovered beading in 1990 and have been a bead addict ever since.

Ocean Dreams was inspired by paintings done by Robert Lyn Nelson and Christian Riese Lassen, two famous painters from Hawaii. Their works are primarily paintings of a cross-section of the ocean. *Ocean Dreams* is done using flat and sculptural peyote stitch. It consists primarily of Delica beads, some size 14/0 seed beads, and the cloisonné fish beads. The entire piece was stitched to a brass ring and then attached to a brass frame. I started it in May of 1997 and worked on it for approximately three hundred hours.

I started with the water section in the middle, then added the waves, then decided to cover the ring in the sky section and on the bottom. Next came the sky and the coral, and finally the fish and seaweed. There was no pattern; for inspiration I had my sea calendars and a couple of sea paintings. I just started with an idea and went with it. Some parts took trial and error. The sky section was done twice and parts of the coral section were done three times. Mostly the piece led me where I needed to go. I would work on it for a while and then spend a couple of days just looking at it. Then I would know what to do next. Even though I live in New Mexico, where desert and mountains dominate, I truly love the ocean. I hope those feelings show in this piece.

Kathy Rice has belonged to the Bead Society of New Mexico and the Bead Mavins. She currently belongs to the Enchanted Beaders. She has taught classes at the Bead Mavins and the Enchanted Beaders meetings for many years. She won second place in a design contest at Southwest America (a beadstore in Albuquerque, New Mexico) and at the Bead Mavins. Her article, "Bead One, Knit Two," containing instructions for a knitted beaded pouch of her own design, was published in the Sept/Oct 1997 issue of Jewelry Crafts Magazine. She works as a computer graphics artist at Sandia National Laboratories in Albuquerque, New Mexico.

Melissa Koval

I always had a yen to make jewelry, and in July, 1996, I finally found beads. I studied for two days with Carol Wilcox Wells at G-Street Fabrics in Rockville, Maryland, and learned to make her *Gilded Cage*. I studied with Cynthia Rutledge, also at G-Street Fabrics.

Though it doesn't always happen, I try to bead every day. I am seriously thinking about trying to raise money to do a documentary on beading, contemporary bead artists, and the bead business. That would really challenge all of my skills and interests.

At first I didn't plan on making jellyfish earrings. Using colored pencils and loom graph paper, I drew what I thought was a really beautiful large crab. I tried making it with square stitch and then tried again with a fringed necklace. Both pieces remain unfinished. I was juggling about twenty gorgeous Delica colors, and it wasn't working the way I wanted. There was something derivative about it. I felt really overwhelmed and went back to the drawing board. I remembered making the *Gilded Cage* with Carol Wells, and how pretty it was even though it was just one color of Delica. That's partly because of the *Gilded Cage's* amazing structure. Fewer colors and a three dimensional structure led me to jellyfish. I like them because they are strangely beautiful creatures. I looked in some reference books at a bookstore, got the image of jellyfish in my brain, and within a week made the earrings. I wanted to use memory to create rather than the picture. I hoped the earrings would be more unique that way and I wouldn't get trapped in some clinical copy. In the end, *Jellyfish Earrings* were made using only three colors of Delicas: DB109, DB64, and DB206. The body was made using two layers of tubular peyote—single and multi-drop. Brick stitch ladders and netting were added for support, and they were embellished with seed pearls and Czech glass beads.

Melissa Koval has a Master of Fine Arts degree in Film and Television Production from New York University (1994). Prior to that she studied black and white photography at the Corcoran School of Art in Washington, D.C. in a non-degree program (1986-1987). Her undergraduate degree is a Bachelor of Science in Electrical Engineering from the University of Pittsburgh (1985). While at "Pitt" she minored in studio arts (painting, drawing, sculpture, etc.).

Cheryl Fuller

The source for my design was a collection of four different cross stitch patterns called *Circles of the Sea*. I combined parts of three of the patterns to create my entry, *Water Colors*. I then adapted the pattern for loom work, doubling it in both directions to get the right size. (The finished piece is twenty-eight inches high.) The hanging rods are burnt wooden dowels with the warp threads tied in little bunches around them. Beading *Water Colors* took almost one hundred ninety hours over a

three-month period, and I nearly didn't finish in time—it took me too long to decide what I wanted to make!

Since completing *Water Colors,* I have prepared a graph for a second half to my hanging. I hope to finish it before too long—but in the meantime I have also started on my entry for the 2nd Delica Challenge.

Patricia Parker

Although I took many art classes in school, I never came across anyone who taught beadwork. Being completely in love with the "small spots of color" that seed beads are, I taught myself to loom weave in 1980 and have been working with seed beads ever since. Most of the techniques I use are learned from books or from looking at a finished piece and figuring out how it was done. I like to "draw" with the beads. I have never met any well-known bead artists, but I am constantly inspired by the ever-growing body of work that contemporary bead artists are creating.

For my entry, *Course Flow or Set of the Waves*, I used a wide variety of techniques. The frame, mermaid, and the fish (with fringe for the fins and tails) are done with square stitch. Unlike loom work, where the loom strings must be factored in, square stitch allows more freedom to shape the beads to the design.

The jellyfish body is a tubular peyote stitch worked around a plastic bead tube with three single-weave netting tail pieces. The crown is two open-weave circles sewn together and then attached to the body with a double square stitch. The tendrils are beads on twisted wire. The jellyfish hangs from a four-bead loop chain.

The starfish is made from a combination of techniques including rosette, ladder stitch, and flat peyote. It was made in two pieces and sewn together.

The sea anemones are buttons covered in a right angle weave with fringe tendrils.

The stars were made by starting with ten beads in a circle, adding three beads between every other bead in the base circle, passing back through the second row and looping one bead to each center (2nd) bead in each of the five sections.

The bubbles are clear round plastic beads. They were covered by tying a thread to the plastic bead, stringing a number of crystal AB Delicas, passing the thread through the center of the plastic bead, then back through the Delicas and continuing in this fashion with additional rows of beads until the plastic bead was covered.

After thinking about the theme for the 1st Miyuki Delica Challenge, I looked up the definitions of "sea" and "wave" in a dictionary and wrote them in the border of a frame drawn in a sketchbook. Seventeen years of <u>National Geographic</u> magazine provided many incredible undersea photographs of creatures I never knew existed (thanks for making me look!). As I studied the photos, my mind transformed some of them into beaded creatures. I drew these onto my sketchbook page and made a graph the size of the beads on the computer. I created the frame using square stitch which allowed the freedom to 'freehand sketch' with the beads as I worked. The piece was designed to be a window hanging.

Patricia Parker majored in fine arts at Kutztown University in Pennsylvania. After college she worked as a photographer and in an art supply store. She spent a number of years in graphic design doing paste-up for ads and layouts for signs. In 1994 she opened her own bead store, The Bead Game, located in New Hope, Pennsylvania, where she teaches classes.

Norma Shapiro

It seems that all of my adult life (I'm now sixty-one) I have been involved in the creative arts including oil painting, pottery, and stained glass. With stained glass, especially with wildlife and nature subjects, I felt I had finally found my calling—the changing effect of light on the colored glass really got me! Soon after beginning to work with stained glass, however, two events occurred which changed my direction. First, back problems made it difficult for me to work with stained glass. Second, my husband and I became involved with ballroom dancing which led to embellishing my clothing with beads and sequins. From there, the jump into beading was quick and easy.

An increasing interest in off-loom weaving prompted me to visit Carol Wilcox Wells' studio while in Asheville for a dance weekend in February, 1997. For the three previous years my beading had consisted of strung, elegant, mostly crystal jewelry which I sold through galleries. The vases shown in Well's book, *Creative Bead Weaving,* said to me, "beautiful, interesting and do-able." Having made several coral reef scenes in stained glass, a vase titled *Coral Reef Scene* seemed the ideal work to meet the theme of the 1st Miyuki Delica Challenge.

I really enjoyed the challenge of making a vase, but this piece should be subtitled: "How not to enter a creative competition!" A three dimensional sculpture and the use of flat spiral and tubular spiral brick stitch were firsts for me. I erroneously thought that the deadline for the competition was August 1st. I knew that I had no free time for beading in July, so I reluctantly put the competition out of my mind. Then, early in August, I realized that the deadline was in fact August 31st! I began getting my psyche and materials together and started working furiously. In retrospect, it seems like I ended every day of the last two weeks of August with the words: "Just a few more hours and this will be finished!" Eventually the wave trim was finished and it was ready to ship—except for a quick visit to the one-hour photo lab for the required photos! Unfortunately there was no time left for the intended three dimensional touches on the corals and sea whips, or to redo some of the little gaps resulting from my inexperience with brick stitch, or to correct some of the shading I attempted by using different colors of thread. At least I can look forward to the next Delica Challenge having learned many important lessons!

Sue Maguire

In January 1995, I attended a day course entitled Bead Embroidery given by Pam Watts, a respected teacher both in the UK and in the USA. Part of the day was spent learning brick stitch to enable us to make an amulet purse. I was hooked and have been beadweaving ever since, teaching myself all the other stitches from books. I incorporated the techniques into the work I was doing for my City and Guilds* exam—one of my final pieces being a beaded panel. I am a member of the Embroiderer's Guild and the Settlement Textile Group. The STG is a small group of past City and Guild students. We meet weekly to encourage each other. Our aim is to produce work for exhibitions, competitions, etc., and to continue to work to a high standard.

Delica Sea is worked in peyote stitch. I had used the pale beads in a previous piece of work and they suggested the translucency of jellyfish to me. I wanted a feeling of the jellyfish drifting through the water trailing their tentacles. I also liked the idea of the inside of the piece being visible as well as the outside, hence the clear glass.

*To give it its proper title, The City and Guilds London Institute is an examinations body which sets exams nationally in many subjects. Successful graduates are awarded certificates. The course I completed was entitled Creative Studies—Embroidery (part 1) and Extended Embroidery Skills (part 2). We studied traditional techniques and British historical embroidery in part 1.

In part 2 we studied embroidery from medieval times to the present day, as well as foreign embroidery. Having mastered the traditional techniques in part 1, part 2 required us to develop a much freer and more modern approach to our own work. It was a fascinating experience and taught me not only about embroidery, but also a lot of history. Although quite structured in some respects, the course was quite flexible and geared to the individual. When I discovered beadweaving I was able to incorporate it into the work I was doing and was encouraged to develop and extend my approach and capabilities.

Nancy Badciong

I'm a medical technologist and work in the chemistry laboratory in a hospital. I don't get to be artistic there, although there is a lot of organization and detail which carries over to beading. In truth, beading is my escape from work.

I started beading three and a half years ago. I've attended two of Carol Wilcox Wells' retreats. The first one covered the *Gilded Cage*; the second one covered the *Cuffed Basket* and *Under the Apple Tree*. In the summer of 1997 I took the Wonder Bead class given by Sue Jackson and Wendy Hubick—the Hummingbeads.

I've had no formal art training except for some photography classes. Studying photography has helped me in the way that I look at the world around me for the details, color, and special things that many people overlook. I also collect photos from magazines and have used them in my beading for color ideas and designs.

The lower portion of *Sea's Crystal Garden* was done in brick stitch which changed to peyote for the major portion of the body. Branched fringe was used for the top of the wave and for the coral/pearl embellishment around the base. The pedestal is circular peyote covered by a layer of Delicas laid into the 'trough' in the peyote cylinder. The bottom of the pedestal was covered with a flat circular peyote piece.

The idea for *Sea's Crystal Garden* came from the book, ***Pass the Butterworms***, by Tim Cahill. In the book Eric Soares tells of a kayaking trip in the Big Sur coastal region. As his kayak passed through the waves, he was enveloped in spray. The sun coming through the spray turned the drops into individual prisms which he called "crystal gardens." As soon as I read this I knew what I wanted to represent.

I had many blue Delicas to choose from to show the colors of the water. Swarovski crystals would be perfect to represent the crystals and colors of the rainbow. Instead of a crashing wave, I would have mine form a circle—flowing into itself with the crystals inside hidden from view, just as the sunlight and spray "crystal garden" described by Soares is hidden from us. My wave falls through several different colors of the sea to a large blue crystal at the bottom. The crystals in the bottom layer have acted as seeds for the coral and pearls visible on the outside. The crystals are the "hidden" garden, but we are able to see the coral gardens beneath the waves.

Juanita Finger

I've had formal musical training and I relate colors to the feelings that music evokes. Intense reds, for example, make me feel the way an intense, angry musical piece makes me feel. I relate both color and music to emotion. Sometimes I see a mix of colors and it makes me think of a design. I once saw a brightly painted ceiling in a restaurant and designed an amulet bag on the paper tablecloth. I tune into the mix of colors and find a depth of emotions and images.

I started beading about seven or eight years ago. I had been given a pair of beaded earrings which broke. Since I had done other crafts such as knitting and crocheting, I felt that I could repair my earrings. I bought some beads and a 'how-to' book. I did repair my earrings and got hooked on beading in the process. I have not taken any classes but I read articles and books which explain how to do each type of stitch. While I haven't formally studied under any well-known artists, I do seek them out when I travel in their areas. I find them friendly and willing to exchange ideas and techniques. Beading is easy to learn and relaxing if you are patient. If you can do macramé, crocheting, or knitting, you can bead!

To make *Lost Pearl,* I used peyote stitch on the pearl and as the base for the mound of seaweed. The pearl has a clear ball center which I covered with a mixture of white delicas. The seaweed base is a green/seafoam cone done in peyote stitch. I covered this cone with a multi-green color branched fringe. This fringe is flowing and conceals the abundance of sea life within its embrace.

When I heard that the theme for the 1st Miyuki Delica Challenge was the sea, I thought of several things. I had recently attended a bead exhibit and seeing so many examples of beading made my mind go wild. I quickly realized, however, that I didn't have the technical knowledge to create the images in my mind. Bringing my ideas to the level of my experience, I came up with a shell and pearl idea. Again my inexperience prevented me from creating the shell. I was at a loss. The solution came in a dream when I saw a lost pearl lying on a bed of seaweed on the ocean floor—at last I had found an image I could recreate in beads.

Deborah Trott

I first picked up beads in the spring of 1986. At that time, I met the Kola family of artists here in Kent, Ohio. ("Kola" is the Lakota word for friend.) Their beadwork was dazzling and beautifully organic. It inspired me to learn beading. I saw beadwork as a highly evolved art form which allows the artist to integrate an infinite variety of elements resulting in a truly unique creation.

My life's journey then took me to the hill country of Tennessee. I stumbled upon a copy of Ornament magazine at the local college library and my love affair with beads was born. I ordered the necessary items by mail, but more importantly, I ordered books which were my teachers now that my bead friends were so far away.

I learned most of what I know through experience and a series of books, *Beads to Buckskins* by Peggy Sue Henry. In particular, I like to work with deerskin, seed beads, organic objects, and beads from all over the world.

Two of my spare time interests, genealogy and mythology, inspired me to depict a dolphin on my entry to the 1st Miyuki Delica Challenge. I wanted to silhouette *Dolphin* on a porcelain-like background, possible only with the help of matte Delicas. I used square stitch to create the main body of the piece.

My maternal family comes from Italy. While reading about the mythology of the ancient Greeks and Italians, I discovered how intertwined these two cultures are. I was fascinated by the art of that period. The dolphin was considered a friendly animal and was even anthropomorphized. Wonderful stories exist about human and dolphin interaction. Since my ancestors lived for centuries on the shores of the Mediterranean, I thought it would be appropriate to commemorate a time when humans and animals were not so wary of each other.

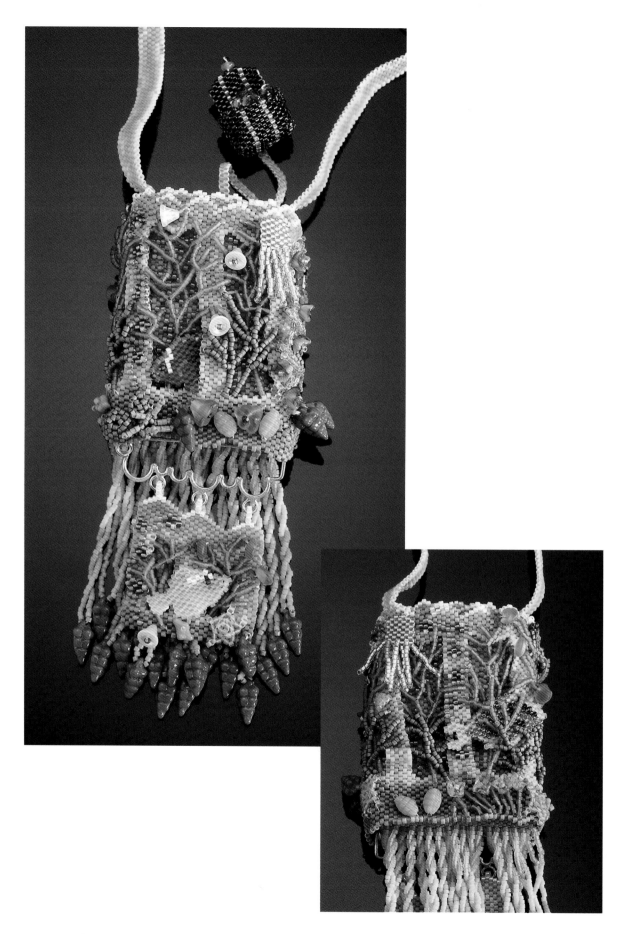

Deborah Stone McCarthy

I'm primarily self-taught but have taken classes with Joyce Scott, Carol Wilcox Wells, Colleen Wilmer, and Ava Motherwell. When I design, I usually start with a general idea and then the beads guide me. The beads and stones know where they want to be. Much of my inspiration comes from nature.

My entry, *Beneath the White Caps*, is a beaded amulet purse with a detachable brooch. It is intended to evoke an underwater fantasy of swimming fish, blooming plants, sea-dwelling animals, and cool ocean currents.

The purse was built by creating multiple layers of beadwork and then connecting them. Once the pieces of the base purse were joined, surface embellishment was added by stitching on additional layers of beadwork and adding individually created ornaments (fish, turtle, jellyfish, brain coral, starfish, and trailing vines with flowers).

The detachable brooch is connected with a sterling silver finding through beaded loops which are hidden behind an apron extending from the bottom of the purse. The brooch has openings in it to allow the twisted fringe of the bag to show through, creating the illusion of the motion of the sea.

The purse was constructed using primarily the peyote stitch in its many forms—tubular and flat, increasing and decreasing, even and odd, and circular. The fish were made using the Comanche stitch, and surface embellishment was added using the square stitch. The bag has twisted fringe on the bottom and uses the basic idea of branched fringe (with the branch ends attached) to create the underwater greenery.

The bag also contains a secret treasure: a beaded chest filled with gold and jewels hides inside the bag for the curious to discover. The treasure chest is attached to the bag with a narrow peyote stitched strap of "water blue" Delica beads.

Deborah Stone McCarthy's neckpiece, The Tree of Life, *won first prize in the First Annual Rainforest Beadwork Contest at Crystal Blue Beading Company in Watertown, Massachusetts, in 1992. Her beaded amulet purses were part of the* Spiritual Vessels *exhibit at Beadworks on Newbury Street in Boston and near Harvard Square in Cambridge, Massachusetts, during the summer of 1995. She is married and lives on the family farm in Sudbury, Massachusetts, with her husband, Dermot, their ten-year-old son, Patrick, their cat, Dunkie, and whatever wildlife happens to wander through.*

Lisa Ring

I started beading about six years ago, making jewelry from freshwater pearls, gemstone beads, and Austrian crystals. In late 1994, I was looking for a new challenge. I started making brick stitch earrings and bought my first Delica beads, which was the beginning of the end. I now have more than one hundred seventy Delica colors and my collection is growing! I fell in love with Jennifer Clement's *Turtles Dancing* amulet bag pattern in the May/June 1995 issue of <u>Bead and Button</u> and decided to learn peyote stitch. Since that time I have made over forty bags. When someone requests a bag, I enjoy the creative process of picking out the perfect design and colors with them. I usually make a test strip of the design and colors for them before starting their bag. My test strip (which includes samples from all my original designs) is now almost two feet long, but it makes a great conversation piece and reference to past projects. Most of my bags are inspired by instruction books, pictures from books, magazines, needlepoint designs, and the Internet. I create my own designs on the computer using a bead grid I developed in the program Corel Draw.

Laguna Moon was created in even count tubular peyote, folded flat with a three bead picot edging on both sides of the bag, sewn shut along the bottom, and two-bead flat peyote strap carriers at the top. It has a single-strand beaded strap strung on Flex-wire. There is a row of fringe around the bottom of the bag. The fringe and strap are constructed of Austrian crystal beads and teardrops, faceted Czechoslovakian glass beads, dichroic glass beads, Miyuki triangle beads and 24kt Charlottes.

Laguna Moon began when a friend wanted a bag with an "ocean" theme. Jennifer Clement's personal untitled bag provided the inspiration for the wave design, and *Japanese Sea* by Carol Wilcox Wells planted the idea to put a moon above the waves. After much experimenting with design and bead colors, *Laguna Moon* was born! It owes its name to Laguna Beach, California, one of my favorite beach towns.

Nancy Jones

My beading career began when I made a trip to Alaska in September, 1994. At an artisan's gallery in Ketchikan there was a display of peyote stitched rope necklaces hanging on a pedestal, glistening in the sun. That was it! I purchased two and examined them the entire trip home because this was what I was going to do. My first beading effort was beading dull green beads around the handle of my crochet hook.

It seemed only appropriate to chronicle the trip up the Inside Passage that inspired the beading frenzy which now consumes my every waking moment. We had drizzle and gray skies the entire week. The dropping-off-into-the-bay, stark, beautiful landscape is what I wanted to project in my entry, *Inside Passage*. The soapstone carving is reminiscent of the totems and native culture. This project came full circle for me since this trip brought the exciting dimension of beads to my art.

Peyote stitch is the basic technique used, along with branched fringe around the carving. Most of my beading so far has been amulet bags, so that was the only realistic choice for the Delica Challenge. My designs are very structured and controlled, symmetrical, and geometric. Silver wire work is incorporated into the handle of the evening bag.

Nancy Jones is self-taught and does all of her own designs. She was featured in the "Your Work" section of the February, 1996 issue of <u>Bead and Button</u> magazine, and has had entries accepted for competition at Embellishment (four in 1996, and two in 1997). Her amulet bags are on display in two bead shops in the Houston area.

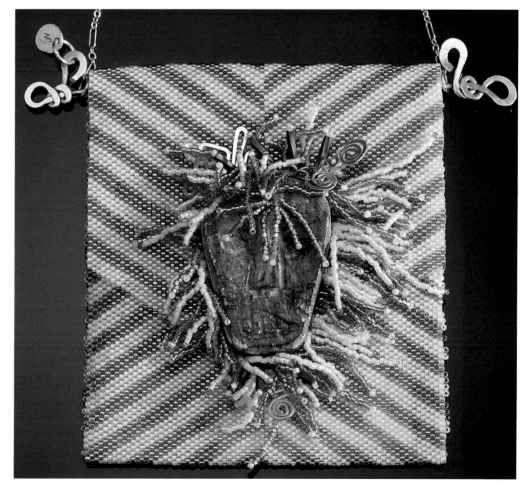

Sheri Nelson

Before starting to bead in 1991, I had done crochet, cross stitch, and embroidery. I actually started beading because my husband wanted a pair of mukluks. I did the beadwork right onto the leather which is quite difficult. To learn beading, I read as many books as I could find and got a lot of tips from other beaders. I have never taken a class, but have now gotten to the point where I teach. I go into various villages and teach different stitches to the Alaskan natives. They do applique mostly, and have asked me to teach the different weaving techniques. I enjoy designing pieces that show Alaskan wildlife.

I used the odd count peyote stitch for my entry. To the branched fringe, I added everything I could find that relates to the sea: shells, fish, pearls, and sea urchin spines. I did little windows in the neck piece and intertwined pearls through them.

I included the killer whales and northern lights because they reflect Alaska. I've watched the whales and their grace reminded me of the lights, so I titled my entry *Dancing to the Lights*.

In the future I hope to organize a beading retreat, mainly for bead lovers to get together and enjoy exchanging ideas and to experience the beauty that we have to offer—Alaska can give lots of inspiration to crafters of any kind.

*Sheri Nelson lives in Central, Alaska. She has won several first, second, and third place awards at the Fairbanks Fair. She also took a division championship for a beaded cabochon hat band. Recently she acquired her first computer to aid her in designing and she has also published her first book, **Alaska in Beads**.*

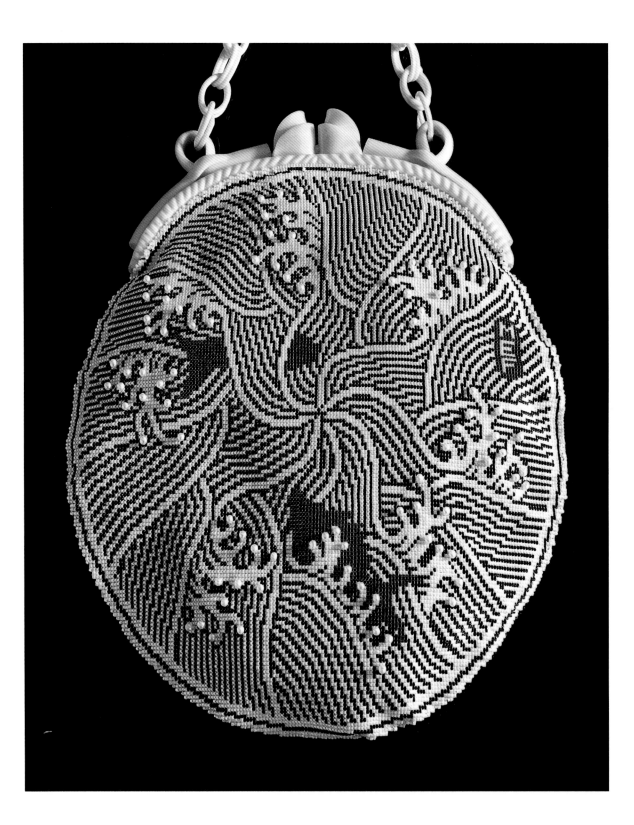

Mary Fraser

My mother and grandmother were both excellent seamstresses who taught me embroidery at an early age. Until I discovered beading, I spent many evenings doing counted cross stitch. Since I started beading two years ago, I haven't stitched another stitch! I find working with seed beads very therapeutic and the amount of time I spend beading proves that I need a lot of therapy!

After seeing some beautiful beadwork in Santa Fe, New Mexico, I took a class on making amulet purses at a local bead shop. I made amulet purses for about a year and then I began making larger purses. I was inspired by a book on antique purses which showed a design that reminded me of a counted stitch pattern. After making several larger purses and estimating the time to make a purse to be about two hundred hours, I decided to look for antique frames to complement the purses. I now have an antique purse collection, belong to a purse club, and spend my weekends attending antique shows.

Spiral Waves was done in square stitch and embellished with freshwater pearls. I do most of my work using square stitch because I like to have pictures on my purses and often use needlepoint patterns. This pattern was adapted for needlepoint from a Ching Dynasty porcelain plate that is at the Worcester Art Museum in Massachusetts. In the case of *Spiral Waves*, I had completed all of the beadwork before I found the purse frame. I was quite pleased to find a frame that was the right color, shape and size. Some people say it was luck, but I say it was persistence!

Caravan Beads

Marcia Katz

I have a bachelor's degree in elementary education with a specialization in art. I have taken art courses at the New School, Radcliffe College, museum schools, and at professional conferences. Some of the best beading techniques I have learned were at local workshops where the classes were small and there was plenty of time to share. I find that some of my best ideas come from networking at our weekly open beading get-togethers. We critique each other's work and teach each other any new techniques we have learned.

Color has always been essential to me, hence my years of collecting beads and beaded handbags. Among other careers, I used to design and knit sweaters for yarn companies when they introduced new yarns at shows, and I taught knitting and sweater design. I actually started working with beads during my years of knitting as many of my designs included feathers and beads. I slowly started using more beads than yarn and became a beadwork artist, although I still use fibers in my woven bead and fiber pieces. I also do a lot of work on a beading loom which I designed for myself and now market commercially.

Deciding what to make for the Delica Challenge came very naturally. I live on the beach and walk the beach every day collecting shells. As soon as I read about the Challenge I knew exactly what I would enter. To make *Festoonery*, I first enclosed the shell in netting. Then I embellished it with free-form sculptured peyote and drilled shells. The neckpiece was constructed using a tubular stitch and embellished with drilled shells.

Marcia Katz belongs to The St. Lucie County Rock and Gem Club and The Gem and Mineral Society of the Palm Beaches. She teaches beading (mostly with seed beads) and fiber-and-bead weaving. She has been hired as an instructor at the Rock and Gem Club, Gem and Mineral Society, The Center for Art and Soul in Stuart, The Studio in Stuart, The Lighthouse Gallery in Tequesta, and will also be teaching beading classes for the staff of The Pavilion of Jupiter Hospital in Jupiter. In 1997, one of her three dimensional loom pieces was juried into the Embellishment competition. She is a founding member of The Treasure Coast Bead Society. Marcia maintains a website at www.festoonery.com.

Helen Karen Wood

I became interested in beading in the late fall of 1996. A beautiful necklace of mine, made of silver chain and colored glass beads, was in need of repair. A friend from California, a professional beader, visited and we spent one rainy Sunday afternoon at the bead store in Princeton designing a new dangle for my necklace. I was smitten.

After making a few necklaces and earrings, I bought books and began to study the designs and compositions. In March of 1997, during one of my visits to the bead store, I saw two little postage stamp sized beaded bags, but they were not for sale. The shop was just starting to offer Delica beads and these tiny amulet bags would be made in a class that very weekend. The class was full but I begged and pleaded and finally they squeezed me in. The class was taught by a visiting bead artist from San Francisco. She told us she had carried her first amulet purse around with her for weeks. I vowed to do the same. By the end of the fourth row, I was hooked. I loved the way the Delica beads came together so perfectly. By the time we left the class, we each had a completed (or nearly completed) mini amulet bag. When I got home, ready to attach the strap, I saw that my bag had come undone at both the top and the bottom. So much the better; I quickly learned to correct mistakes. I started another immediately so I wouldn't forget the technique and I haven't stopped since. I have made nineteen to date.

Sea Horse Fantasea was done in even count peyote stitch. I started it by making drawings, sketches, and colored graphs. I spent considerable time trying to get my sea horse to a scale that would fit on an amulet bag and still allow the detail I wanted in the curve of his tail and on his dorsal fin. I determined that maximum size would be one hundred Delicas around (fifty front and fifty back) and one hundred ten rows high. Although the bag would be a little larger than most I had seen, I thought that the size would allow good proportion of height to width. I marked these measurements on my graph pad to remind myself of what the final size would be. I was especially pleased that the final size could hold a beautifully colored silk square, treasure objects and memorabilia, credit cards, or personal business cards.

I constantly changed the design as I found some things that worked and some that didn't. There were many lessons learned from this bag about lines and curves. Working with color was also very much on my mind, not only in terms of the colors used in the bag, but also because using clear crystal beads allowed me to modify the bag's appearance depending on the colors of objects placed in the purse. I designed the front first and allowed the back to develop as a reverse image as I beaded. Many rows (at least another bag's worth) were repeatedly taken out until each was put in as well as I could. The graph was changed so many times that I had to tape many layers of graph paper onto the original. The final one would show the few minor changes I still wanted to make but I felt I had to move along or this sea horse would have only its beautiful tail and would never be entered in the 1st Miyuki Delica Challenge.

Helen Karen Wood was born and raised in northern New Jersey where she studied art for four years. She presently works for a firm that designs home textiles.

Jane Davis *3rd Prize*

I did some beading in the 1970s, then stopped until this year, when a friend showed me some amulet bags she had made. After finding a bead store, Creative Castle, in Newbury Park, I made a bag for my niece for her birthday, and was hooked on beading. This is also where I heard about the 1st Miyuki Delica Challenge. Intending to enter quilt contests this year, I added this entry form to my pile of "things to do."

As soon as I saw the entry form, I decided to make a mermaid. Originally planning to cover a small treasure chest with beads, I was soon caught up in other deadlines and that idea never took shape. As the weeks went by, I mentally gave up on entering, wondering how I would fit in the time to make an entry. One and a half weeks before the entry deadline, I finished my other pending quilting projects and looked through my pile of contest entry forms. (I had been planning on entering another quilt contest but that deadline had passed.)

On the spur of the moment, I sketched the design for the mermaid on canvas, stretched it in my quilting hoop and began sewing on beads for the mermaid's face. That was the start of a week and a half marathon of all-nighters and frantic trips to the bead store to get just the right colors to complete the project. I had planned to couch the beads down, but found that unless I stitched between every bead, they would pop up, so about half way through the piece I switched to back stitch which I liked much better. The tiny shells in the necklace the mermaid is making are from a beach in Hawaii, on Molikai Island. My husband and I went there in 1981 and I spent a whole day with my face practically in the sand finding the smallest little shells I'd ever seen, not knowing what I'd ever do with them but having fun finding them just the same.

Ocean Artisan was a constantly developing work. I had to make decisions every step of the way. And I was trying to think of a title for it all the while. At one point, after deciding the mermaid would be making something in beads (when I had gotten so tired I was silly), my husband had to talk me out of putting little necklaces on all the animals in the piece, as if this little mermaid had gotten carried away and made a beaded necklace for each fish in the sea. (I guess it was a reflection of what I do when I delve into a craft form.) Twice my ten-year-old son knocked my neatly ordered tray of beads all over our carpet. Then, just as I was stopping early one morning, I knocked my beads all over the carpet too! But I was determined to complete this project and submit it to the contest, and although it was grueling to the end, I love working with beads and enjoyed every sleepy, frantic minute of it. Some of my best ideas seem to materialize under pressure, then it's a question of whether I can get them done in time. It worked out this time, but for the next Miyuki Delica Challenge I'm beginning a little earlier!

Jane Davis was born and raised in Southern California. She has a Bachelor of Fine Arts degree in drawing and painting from California State University at Long Beach. She lives in Ventura, California with her husband and three children (all boys, ages ten, eight, and four). She writes quilting instruction booklets part-time, and has, since the Delica Challenge, begun teaching beading at local stores.

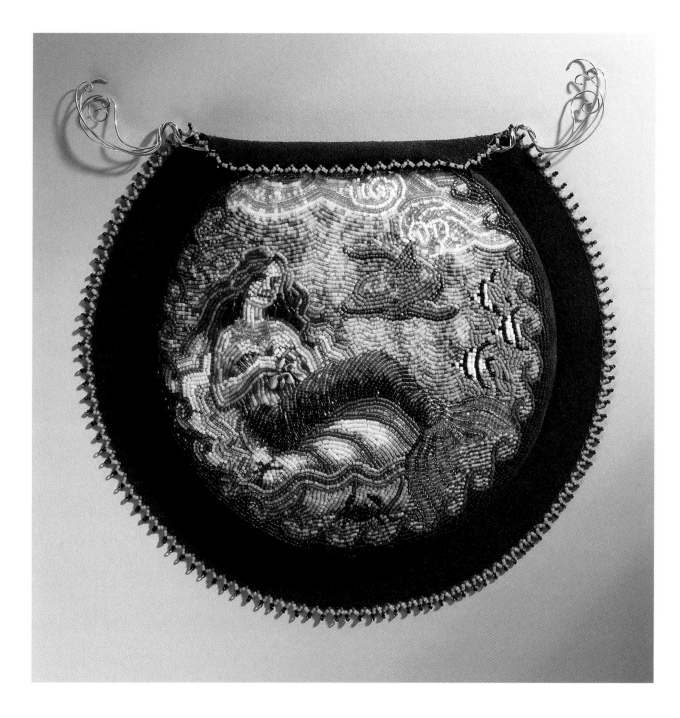

Jane Tyson

I started beading in South Australia. Ironically I took a three lesson crash course in beading the fortnight before we left South Australia to return to Tasmania. Having been 'hooked' on beading, I turned over our local library for books on the subject and nearly despaired. There was so little available. However, by getting hold of a couple of books, I was able to get other titles and sources of books and beads. I now have more than one hundred books and magazines. Most of my beading knowledge comes from books and the Internet.

I also have helped arrange two visits to Australia by bead artist and teacher, NanC Meinhardt. Her visits have helped promote beadwork in this country where it is still not a particularly well known art/craft. She has been a great inspiration to me.

My entry was designed to consist of several sections which would be joined with beaded beads. I like my beadwork to be functional which is why I chose to make a necklace. I also prefer the professional look which commercial fittings give to beadwork so I made sure that all the elements could be joined with commercial fittings.

My entry consists mainly of loom work. The fringed loom work technique was adapted from a book by Diane Fitzgerald. I alternated a row of warp beads and a row of loomed beads between each fringe row. Only warp beads are on the outside edges of the loom work so that a tube fitting could be attached to it. I used peyote/gourd stitch to cover the beads and unfinished square stitch for the fish in the centerpiece. Unfinished square stitch has the tessellated appearance suitable for fish scales. The braided sections were completely loomed and finished off before being braided. The technique for this comes from Wendy Simpson Conner's *Best Little Beading Book*.

A good deal of thought went into my entry, *Deep Dreams*. Man's association with the sea extends to many levels. I chose to look at it in terms of the surface, the middle and the bottom of the sea. On the surface, there are waves and hints of blue and the occasional fish. The blue/white fringing is reminiscent of seaweed and surf. Under the surface there are the well known sea animals. At the bottom of the sea, there is not much to see except the lights sometimes generated by animals. I chose to depict this as blue/violet beads in keeping with an imaginary rather than 'real' vision of the sea. Finally, I made the beaded beads to connect the various levels of the sea.

The 2nd International Miyuki Delica Challenge

We plan to sponsor bead design competitions every other year. This book pays tribute to the 1st Miyuki Delica Challenge. Information about the 2nd Delica Challenge is outlined below; to obtain the complete rules and entry forms, see the contact information at the bottom of the page.

Theme: Myths and Folktales of the World

Deadline for receipt of entries: 6 PM, Friday April 2nd, 1999

Judging: April 16th & 19th, 1999

Judges: Carol Wilcox Wells, Diane Fitzgerald, Charlene Coutre Steele

The 2nd Delica Challenge will have three categories:

a) Sculptural, three dimensional, freestanding pieces

b) Framed pieces, tapestries, hanging/wall pieces

c) Body adornment (jewelry, amulet purses)

Prizes will be:

Grand Prize (1 award) - $1,000

Best of Category (3 awards, one in each category) - $500 each

Honorable Mention (3 awards, one in each category) - $150

Judge's Choice (3 awards, from any category) - $75

Employee's Choice (1 award, at the discretion of Caravan Beads' employees and judges) - $50

Complete rules and entry forms are available by writing to:

Caravan Beads, Inc.

449 Forest Ave.

Portland, ME 04101 USA

207-761-2503 fax: 207-874-2664

You may email your request to: info@caravanbeads.com. (Please include your snail mail address.)

Download the information from our web site: www.caravanbeads.com. (The contest information link is on the main index page.)

Or visit your local beadstore. If they don't have the entry forms, please let us know.

We've even chosen a theme for the 3rd Challenge. Since it will be judged in the year 2001, we've titled it **2001: Out of this World.**

Common beadweaving stitches

This introduction to some of the most widely used beadweaving stitches is deliberately as brief and simple as we could make it. (For more detailed information please refer to the suggested reading at the end of this section.) Nonetheless, a beginner following these instructions should get a feeling for the various stitches, how they differ, and how they are used. You'll need some beads (we've drawn Delicas which are cylindrical, uniform, and have large holes—all of which make them easy to use—but any reasonably uniform seed beads will do for experimenting), thread (Nymo or Silamide are commonly used; check your local bead store or the Delica sources at the end of the book) and beading needles (#12 is best for all-around use). In the instructions below, assume that you will leave a 6-inch length of thread as a tail when starting each stitch. Some beaders also like to tie on an anchor bead when beginning which is not counted as part of the work.

Peyote Stitch

Peyote stitch has been around for ages. Its most basic forms are tubular and flat, each of which can be executed with an even or odd number of beads. A cardboard paper towel tube or similar object can be used to provide support when starting tubular peyote. Figure 1 shows a top view of a row of tubular peyote.

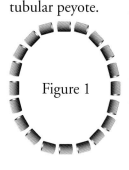

Figure 1

Even count tubular peyote stitch begins with an even number of beads on the first row. The pink thread in Figure 2 shows the beginning of the second row (pass the needle through the first bead after the knot, add a new bead, then go through the third bead, etc.) Figure 3 shows how the second row of beads continues and how the beads line up. (The drawings show spaces between the beads. When you actually work the stitches, the beads touch.) Orange thread in Figure 4 shows how to add in the third row of beads. The first few rows are the hardest. Once those are done the piece will begin to support itself and the cardboard tube can be removed.

If you're making a purse or other flexible piece, leave an empty space equal to two or three beads on the first row. Use a couple of square knots to tie it off.

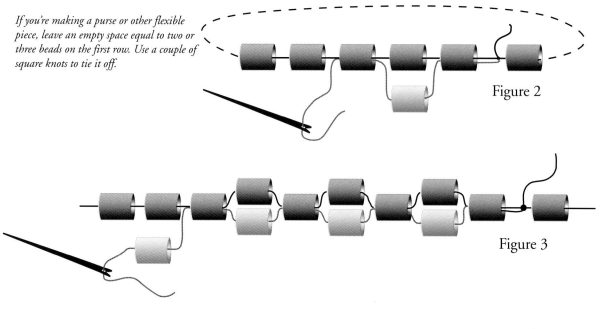

Figure 2

Figure 3

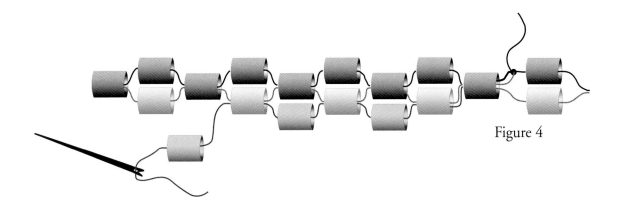

Figure 4

Odd count tubular peyote, as the illustrations show, looks very much like even count peyote at the beginning. Once you get your piece underway, however, you will discover that it moves down the tube or other support in a spiral pattern. We've marked the first bead in each row with a star.

Start with an odd number of beads. Two contrasting colors of the larger 8/0 Delicas will give you a quick feeling for how the stitches look and the big beads are easy to manipulate.

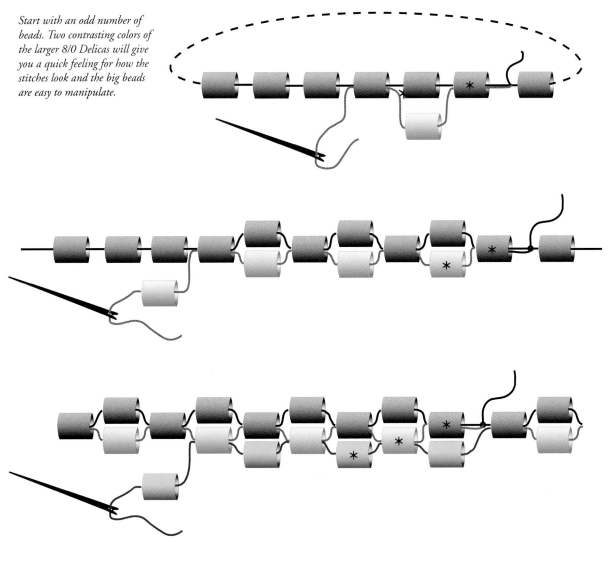

Even count flat peyote is illustrated in figures 1 and 2.

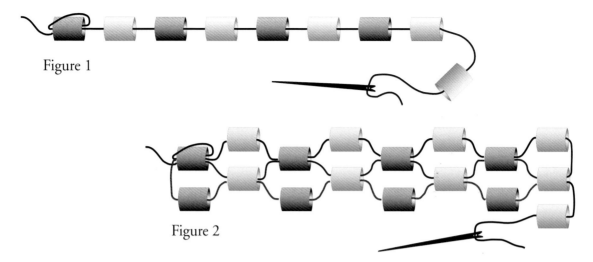

Figure 1

Figure 2

Odd count flat peyote differs from even count not only by having an odd number of beads in each row, but more importantly in how you make your turn at the end of the rows. On one side of the piece, use the simple turn shown on the right in figure 4. This is the same as the turns shown above in even count flat peyote.

Figure 3

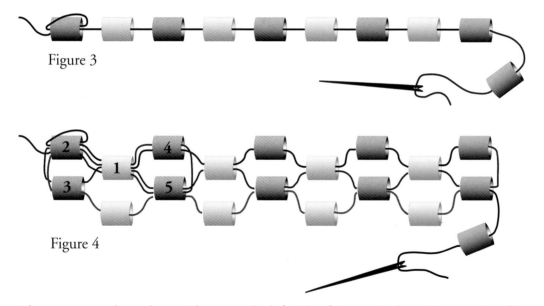

Figure 4

The more complicated turn (shown at the left side of Figure 4, above) is actually a figure eight. It begins as the 'pink' thread passes through bead 1 and continues through beads 2 and 3. Then it re-enters bead 1, picks up 4 and 5, and finally passes through beads 1 and 3 to complete the figure eight.

Note that while the figure eight turn illustrated in figure 4 involves the last three vertical rows of beads, that is only true at the beginning of your piece. Starting with the fourth row, the turn (shown at right) passes through beads in the last two vertical rows..

Right Angle Weave

This technique forms a flexible fabric which can be folded, bent, or draped. Worked flat it forms a sheet. If the last unit is connected to the first, it becomes a tube. It can also be worked to conform to regular or irregular shapes.

Figure 1 shows the basic four bead unit. (Knot the first group.) Note that the thread goes through the first unit in a clockwise direction and then reverses to counter-clockwise for the next four beads. This reversal of direction continues throughout.

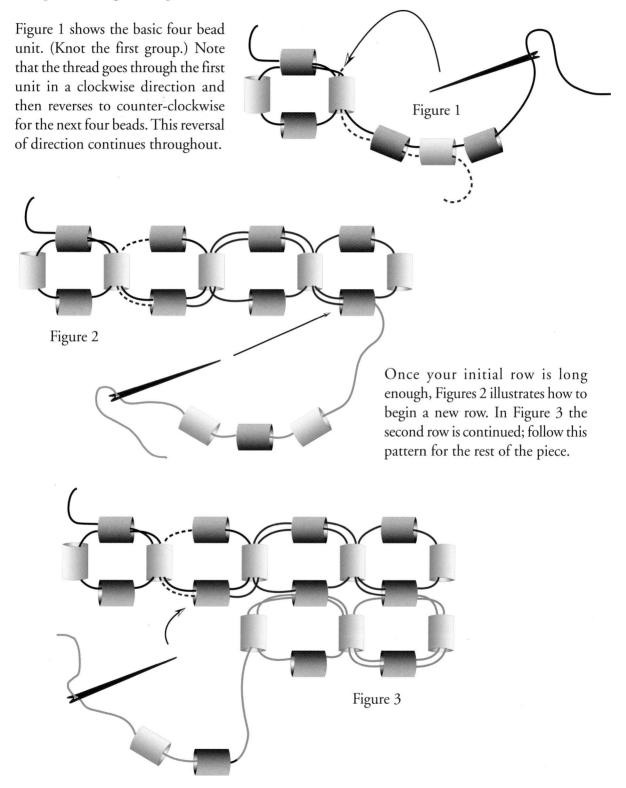

Figure 1

Figure 2

Once your initial row is long enough, Figures 2 illustrates how to begin a new row. In Figure 3 the second row is continued; follow this pattern for the rest of the piece.

Figure 3

Flat Comanche or Brick Stitch

Like peyote stitch, Comanche or brick stitch is another ancient beading technique. It starts with a foundation or ladder row from which the rest of the piece is suspended.

Thread on two beads and pass the needle back through them twice as shown by the black thread in Figure 1. Thereafter pick up each new bead and loop twice through the previous one (pink thread). Repeat until the ladder is the length you need.

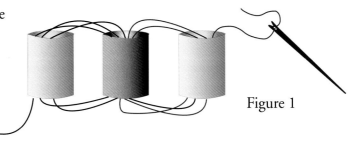

Figure 1

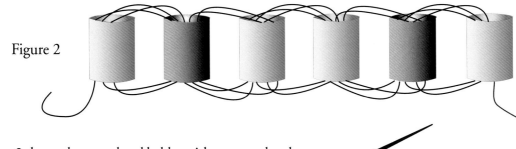

Figure 2

Figure 2 shows the completed ladder with two new beads in place to begin the second row. The pink thread in Figure 3 shows how to loop over the connecting thread in the ladder. Adjust the position of the new beads and then pass the needle back through the last bead. Once the turn is made, beads are added one at a time. Figure 4 shows a completed section.

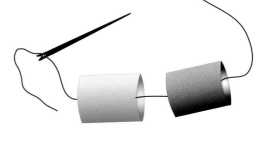

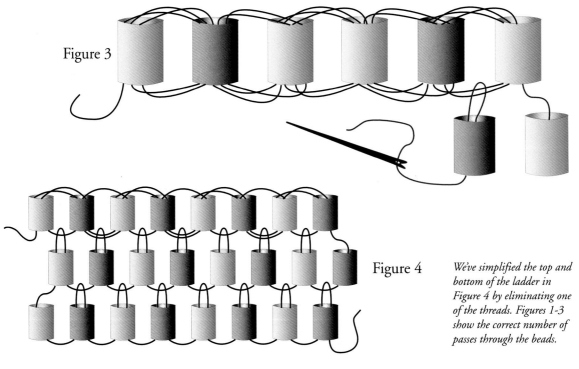

Figure 3

Figure 4

We've simplified the top and bottom of the ladder in Figure 4 by eliminating one of the threads. Figures 1-3 show the correct number of passes through the beads.

Square Stitch

The vertical and horizontal alignment of the beads in square stitch gives finished pieces the appearance of loom work. The multiple passes of thread through the beads make it very strong, but also result in a somewhat rigid final product. Figure 1 shows the first row and how to do the turn. (Pick up a bead, go through the bead above it, and repeat on down the row.)

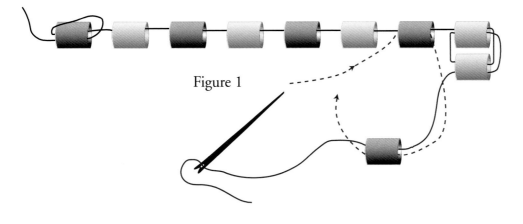

Figure 1

Figure 2 shows the completed second row. To strengthen the work, pass the needle all the way along the first row and all the way back through the second row. (Shown by the green thread in Figure 3.) Now you are ready to pick up a bead and make the turn to begin row three.

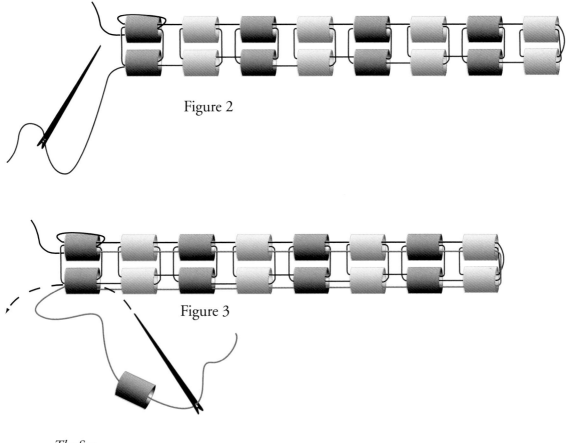

Figure 2

Figure 3

Recommended Reading

Whether you are interested in how-to books, the history of beads, or just want to drool on gorgeous photos, there are a lot more beading books to choose from now than there were even a few years ago. Add to this the explosion of beading information on the Web, and it is clear that the new beader—rather than struggling to find any information—is likely to find too much. As with other information explosions, however, quantity and quality are two different animals. The sources below are ones we have found useful both personally and to our retail customers, but they are merely the tip of the bead information iceberg.

General information and history:

Dubin, Lois Sherr. *The History of Beads*. NY: Harry N. Abrams, Inc., 1987.

Liu, Robert K. *Collectible Beads*. Vista, CA.: Ornament, 1995.

Mack, John, ed. *Ethnic Jewelry*. NY: Harry N. Abrams, 1994.

Moss, Kathlyn, and Alice Scherer. *The New Beadwork*. NY: Harry N. Abrams, 1992.

General beading, recommended for beginners:

Coles, Janet, and Robert Budwig. *The Book of Beads*, NY: Simon & Schuster, 1990.

Conner, Wendy Simpson. *The Best Little Beading Book*. La Mesa, CA: Interstellar Publishing Co., 1997.

Nelson, Teresa and Kathy Christenson. *Beading Frenzy*. Canby, OR: Hot Off the Press, 1993.

Spears, Therese. *Flash Jewelry Making and Repair Techniques*. Boulder, CO: Promenade Publishing, 1990.

For Delica lovers in particular and seed bead lovers in general:

Cooper, Suzanne. *Dancing Light*. Spring Branch, TX: Suzanne Cooper, Inc., 1995.

Cooper, Suzanne. *Uniquely Yours*. Spring Branch, TX: Suzanne Cooper, Inc., 1996.

Elbe, Barbara. *Back to Beadin'*. Redding, CA: B.E.E. Publishing, 1996.

Elbe, Barbara. *Amulet Obsession*. Redding, CA: B.E.E. Publishing, 1998.

Preslar, Pam, *A Beadworker's Toolbook*. Tucson, AZ: Polar Publishing Co., 1995.

Stessin, Nicolette. *Beaded Amulet Purses*. Seattle, WA: Beadworld Publishing, 1994.

Wells, Carol Wilcox. *Creative Bead Weaving*. Asheville, NC: Lark Books, 1996.

Wynne-Evans, Sigrid. *Magic Amulet Bag, Vol.2*. Campbell, CA: Beaded Bear Publishing, 1997.

Periodicals

Check your local beadstore, bookstore or library for these. Phone numbers are for subscription information.

Bead and Button. 800-400-2482

Beadwork. 800-645-3675

Jewelry Crafts. 800-528-1024

Lapidary Journal. 800-676-4336

Ornament. 800-888-8950

On the World Wide Web:

Beadnet <www.mcs.net/~simone/beadnet.html> has links to hundreds of bead-related sites. Suzanne Cooper's site <www.suzannecooper.com> is more manageable in scope and offers links to the sites of some extremely talented bead artists. Be prepared for hours of exploration!

North American Retail Sources for Miyuki Delicas

We hope this list will make it easier for readers to find local Delica sources, and also assist travelers looking for new shops to visit. We've included all the sources we know of, but have, inevitably, missed others. If you own a bead store or retail mail order business that sells Miyuki Delicas and are not on this list, please contact us. We'll be happy to add your information to the next printing of this book and to our web site.

Alabama

Soho South
PO Box 1324
Cullman, AL 35056-1324
205-739-6114
soho@airnet.net
showroom by appt. (catalog $2.50)

Beads!
The Plaza at Riverchase
1845 Riverchase Plaza
Hoover, AL 35244
205-402-0555

Alaska

Alaska Bead Co.
2217 E Tudor Rd. Suite 7
Anchorage, AK 99507
907-563-2323
beadpicker@customcpu.com
retail & mail order (catalog $3.00)

Black Elk, Inc.
5911 Old Seward Hwy.
Anchorage, AK 99518
907-562-2703

Pristine's
1255 Airport Way Suite 10A
Fairbanks, AK 99701
907-479-7122

Arizona

Double Joy Beads
7121 E. Sahuaro Dr.
Scottsdale, AZ 85254
602-998-4495
800-497-3702
hkxb59@prodigy.com
retail & mail order

Arkansas

Mountain Beadery
1621 East Oak St.
Conway, AR 72032
501-327-9335
800-679-7278
retail & mail order (free catalog)

California

Heart Bead
761 8th St.
Arcata, CA 95521
707-826-9577

Out On A Whim
121 E. Cotati Ave.
Cotati, CA 94931
707-664-8343

Jewelart
1811 East Dakota
Fresno, CA 93726
209-229-4066

Oskadusa
243 N. Highway 101
Solana Beach, CA 92075
619-755-2323

3 Beads & A Button
10555 E. Estates
Cupertino, CA 95014
408-366-2323
3beads@ihot.com

The Black Bead
5003 Newport Ave.
San Diego, CA 92107
619-222-2115

Bead Asylum
5692 Thornton Ave.
Newark, CA 94560
510-744-0514

Creative Castle
2321 Michael Dr.
Newbury Park, CA 91320
805-499-1377
www.netresult.com/creativecastle
retail & mail order

Beads Beads
949 N. Tustin Ave.
Orange, CA 92867
714-639-1611

Kelly Trading Co.
1191 Magnolia St., Suite D
Corona, CA 91719
909-270-0686

Gotsie's
207 5th St.
Huntington Beach, CA 92648
714-969-7000

Bead World
17300 17th St.
Tustin, CA 92680
714-838-5134

Colorado

Desert Gems
7100 N. Broadway
Denver, CO 80221
303-426-4411

Pearls and Jewels Bead Shop
1457A South Pearl St.
Denver, CO 80210
303-744-6944

South Park Pottery
P.O. Box 459
Fairplay, CO 80440
719-836-2698
prd@chaffee.net
retail & mail order

Beyond Beadery
PO Box 460
Rollinsville, CO 80474
303-258-9389
beyondbead@aol.com
http://members.aol.com/beyondbead
mail order or by appt. (catalog $2.00)

Connecticut

Harvest
44 Oak St.
Manchester, CT 06040
860-649-2908

Beadoir, Inc.
951A Farmington Ave.
W. Hartford, CT 06107
860-231-8755

District of Columbia

Beadazzled
1507 Connecticut Ave. NW
Washington, DC 20036
202-265-2323

Florida

The Bead String
2932-1 University Blvd., W.
Jacksonville, FL 32217
904-448-9888

Peace Creek Trading Co., Inc.
222 E. Pine St.
Lakeland, FL 33801
941-686-5562
peacecrk@gte.net

Bead Bar
1319 Edgewater Dr.
Orlando, Fl 32804
407-426-8826

Florida (cont.)

Imagine That!
1474 W. Granada Blvd #420
Ormond Towne Square
Ormond Beach, FL 32174
904-673-1202
beadone@aol.com

Beads, F.O.B.
2312 Gulf Gate Dr.
Sarasota, FL 34231
941-921-0871
Beadsfob@aol.com
www.sungate.com/beadsfob

Crystal Creations
4535 Summit Blvd.
West Palm Beach, FL 33415
561-686-1139

Georgia

Beadazzles
290 Hilderbrand Dr.
Atlanta, GA 30328
404-843-8606

Hawaii

Bead It!
1154 Koko Head Ave.
Honolulu, HI 96816
808-734-1182
beadword@aol.com
retail & mail order

Illinois

Caravan Beads
3350 N. Paulina
Chicago, IL 60657
773-248-9555
caravan@ripco.com
www.caravan.chi.il.us

Ayla's Originals
1020 Water St.
Evanston, IL 60201
847-328-4040

The Gypsy's Bead Shoppe
117 W. State St.
Geneva, IL 60134
630-208-1663

The Bead Boutique Inc.
499 Pennsylvania Ave.
Glen Ellyn, IL 60137
630-545-0628
BeadSmart@aol.com
retail & mail order

Beauty & the Beads
701 N. Milwaukee Ave., Suite 136
Vernon Hills, IL 60061
847-680-6565

Indiana

Just Beads
328 State Rd. 144
PO Box 456
Bargersville, IN 46106
317-422-5006
tbeads@scican.net
retail & mail order (catalog $2.00)

Dazzlers, Inc.
4215 Grape Rd.
Mishawaka, IN 46545
219-277-4438

Iowa

Dawn's Hide & Bead Away
521 E. Washington
Iowa City, IA 52240
319-238-1566

Lousiana

Baton Rouge Bead Co.
15959 Hewwood, Suite F
Baton Rouge, LA 70816
504-755-1332
retail & mail order
$1.00 price list

Maine

The Beadin' Path
231 U.S. Rt. 1
Freeport, ME 04032
207-865-4785

Caravan Beads, Inc.
449 Forest Ave.
Portland, ME 04101
207-761-2503
orders: 800-230-8941
sales@caravanbeads.com
www.caravanbeads.com

Maryland

Beadazzled
501 North Charles St.
Baltimore, MD 21201
410-837-2323

Forest Heart Studio
200 S. Main St. Box 112
Woodsboro, MD 21798
301-845-4447

Fantasy Beads
11254 Triangle Lane
Wheaton, MD 20902
301-933-8411

Massachusetts

Bead Emporium
590 Main St.
Hyannis, MA 02601
508-790-0005
retail & mail order
$1.00 catalog

The Bead Tree
67 Blacksmith Shop Rd.
Box 682
West Falmouth, MA 02574
508-548-4665
beadtree@aol.com
retail & mail order (catalog $2.00)

Crystal Blue Bead Co.
565 Mount Auburn St.
Watertown, MA 02172
617-923-2337

Bead Art Resources
857 Washington St.
Newtonville, MA 02160
617-527-8566

Michigan

Findings, Inc.
2366 E. Stadium Blvd.
Ann Arbor, MI 48104
313-677-8420
findings@mail.ic.net
retail store

Bohemian Beads
22266 Michigan Ave.
Dearborn, MI 48124
313-791-0018
mslarson@msn.com

Bedlam Beadworks
263 West 9 Mile
Ferndale, MI 48220
810-541-8827

Plymouth Beading
550 Forest Ave.
Plymouth, MI 48170
313-451-7410
Plymouth@mich.com
www.mich.com/~plymouth/beading.html
retail & mail order (free price list)

Miner's Den
3417 Rochester Rd.
Royal Oak, MI 48073
248-585-6950

Tradewinds Antiques & Beads
336 N. Main
Watervliet, MI 49098
616-463-8281
twlarry@cybersol.com
www.angelfire.com/biz/twind
retail & mail order, free catalog

Minnesota
Stormcloud Trading Co.
725 Snelling Ave. North
St. Paul, MN 55104
612-645-0343
BeadStorm@aol.com
retail & mail order
catalog $5.00 (refundable)

Minnesota (cont.)

Bobby Bead
1608 West Lake St.
Minneapolis, MN 55408
612-824-8281
toll-free: 888-900-2323
bead-natic@msn.com
retail & mail order

Beautiful Beads
115 Hennepin Ave.
Minneapolis, MN 55401
612-333-0170

Karen Buell Designs Needlework
301 1st St. South
Virginia, MN 55792
218-749-6115
retail store
also mail order:
Karen Buell Designs
303 Lake View Dr.
Hoyt Lakes, MN 55750
218-225-3102
kdbuell@orangenet.com

Missouri

Veon Creations
3565 St. Rd. V
DeSoto, MO 63020
314-586-5377
veonbds@jcn1.com
retail & mail order
$4.00 catalog

Terranean Designs
1771 S. Fremont
Springfield, MO 65804
417-889-2402
800-280-2402
BEADI@aol.com
retail & mail order

Nebraska

Threads
5221 S. 48th St.
Lincoln, NE 68516
402-489-9550
800-248-8959

Ann Evans Gilbert
2621 South 79th St.
Lincoln, NE 68506
402-484-7545
BDMGSteve@aol.com
by appointment

Nevada

Beads, Findings & Jewelry
4001 S. Decatur S-17
Las Vegas, NV 89103
702-871-8450

New Hampshire

Caravan Beads
2 Ridge St.
Dover, NH 03820
603-749-8855

New Jersey

TWE/BEADS
PO Box 55
Hamburg, NJ 07419-0055
973-209-1517
cb@twebeads.com
www.twebeads.com
mail order, free catalog
retail store (call for hours) at:
Viking Village, Rt. 94, McAfee, NJ

New Mexico

Southwest America
1506-C Wyoming NE
Albuquerque, NM 87112
505-299-1856

Arts & Crafts Mart
2717 San Mateo NE
Albuquerque, NM 87110
505-881-2777

Western Traders
1300 El Paseo Suite D3
Las Cruces, NM 88001
505-527-1470
westrad@greatwhite.com

New York

Accents Bead Shop
513 Elmwood Ave.
Buffalo, NY 14222
716-884-4689
accents513@msn.com

The Bead Gallery
3963 Main St.
Buffalo, NY 14226
716-836-6775
www.beadgallery.com

All About Beads
384 New York Ave.
Huntington, NY 11743
516-425-2323
retail & mail order
$3.50 catalog

York Novelty Import
10 West 37th St.
New York, NY 10018
212-594-7040
yorkbead@aol.com
www.yorkbeads.com
retail & mail order (free catalog)

Saratoga Beads
80 Henry St.
Saratoga Springs, NY 12866
518-584-7733

Woodstock Bead Emporium
54 Tinker St.
Woodstock, NY 12498
914-679-0066
retail & mail order
beads@ulster.net
catalog free w/ order

North Carolina

Carol Wilcox Wells
Love to Bead, Inc.
PO Box 8492
Asheville, NC 28814
704-252-0274

Chevron Trading Post & Bead Co.
40 N. Lexington Ave.
Asheville, NC 28801
800-881-2323

Bead Merchants of Charlotte
9926 Providence Forest Ln.
Charlotte, NC 28270
704-843-5509

Caravan Beads
The Cotton Exchange
307 N. Front St.
Wilmington, NC 28401
910-343-0500

Ohio

Isle of Beads
2483 Lee Blvd.
Cleveland Heights, OH 44118
216-371-0173
aa472@seorf.ohiou.edu
mail order only ($2.00 catalog)

Discount Bead House
PO Box 186-B
The Plains, OH 45780
800-793-7592
mail order

Oregon

The Bead Studio
14 S. First St.
Ashland, OR 97520
541-488-3037

The Bead Garden
1313 Mill St. SE
Salem, OR 97302
503-391-9285

South West Trading Post
234 Liberty N.E.
Salem, OR 97301
503-364-4668

Pennsylvania

My Father's Beads
634 N.W. End Blvd.
Quakertown, PA 18951
215-536-6511
smitte@voicenet.com

Le Petit Artist
422 Walnut St.
Reading, PA 19601
610-478-8400

Earth Rhythms
641 Penn Ave.
W. Reading, PA 19607
610-374-3730

Tennessee

The Samplery
2502 Peavine Rd.
Fairfield Glade, TN 38558
615-484-0877

Cindy's Crafts
2532 Elizabethton Hwy.
Johnson City, TN 37601
423-926-0050

Blue Moon Beads
90-A Ogden Lane
Oak Ridge, TN 37830
423-482-5158

Texas

Suza Bead Co.
3516 HWY 6
Sugar Land, TX 77479
281-980-9050

Utah

Beaded Puma
1227 East 330 South, Suite H
Salt Lake City, UT 84106
801-466-5607

Virginia

Juel's Beads and Adornments
7441 Richmond Rd.
Williamsburg VA 23188
757-566-2011
beadornd@widowmaker.com
retail & mail order
pricelist free with S.A.S.E.

Two Feathers
101 Waters Lane
Dumfries, VA 22026
703-221-5622
2feathers@erols.com
www.erols.com/2feathers
retail & mail order (catalog $2.00)

Beadazzled
Tysons Corner Center 1
McLean, VA 22102
703-848-2323

Star's Beads, Ltd.
139A Church St. N.W.
Vienna, VA 22180
703-938-7018
smcgivern@aol.com

Washington

Beads & Beyond
25 102nd Ave. N.E.
Bellevue, WA 98004
425-462-8992
retail & mail order

Blue Iris Beads
222 1st Ave. South
Kent, WA 98032
253-852-8055

Shipwreck Beads
2727 Westmoor Ct S.W.
Olympia, WA 98502
360-754-2323
retail and mail order

Imagine That!
19740-E 7th Ave. N.E.
Poulsbo, WA 98370
360-779-3345

B & B Beads
14607 1st Ave. South
Seattle, WA 98168
206-246-2772
retail and mail order

Empyrean Beads
7129 34th Ave. S.W.
Seattle, WA 98126
206-937-4146
www.overpass.com/empyrean.html
mail order

Wisconsin

Turtle Island Beads
124 3rd St.
Baraboo, WI 53913
608-356-8823
turtle@baraboo.com
mail order/studio open by appt.
free price list

Eclectica
18920 W. Bluemound Rd. #25
Brookfield, WI 53045
414-641-0910

Bead Faeries
1224 Washington St.
Manitowoc, WI 54220
920-683-8412

Knot Just Beads
8000 W National Ave.
West Allis, WI 53214
414-771-8360

Midwest Beads
17700 Capitol Dr.
Brookfield, WI 53045
414-781-7670

CANADA

That Bead Lady
175 Crossland Gate
Newmarket, Ontario L3X 1A7
tel/fax: 905-853-6179
clampole@netcom.ca
mail order only, catalog available

Armure Studios
57 McGee St.
Toronto, Ontario
Canada M4M 2L1
416-463-3815
armure1@pathway1.pathcom.com

The Bead Store
2404 Marine Dr.
West Vancouver, B.C. Canada V7V IL3
604-922-7310